JESUS HELP ME

HAVE PEACE

Ten Proven Practices to Overcome Anxiety and Stress

BY

JAKE HUFFMAN

I dedicate this book to my loving wife, Dana,
my partner in knowing Jesus and making Him known.

Table of Contents

INTRODUCTION...1

SECTION ONE: THE PRINCIPLES

CHAPTER 1: Anxiety and Stress...9
CHAPTER 2: The Principles of Peace............................... 23

SECTION TWO: THE PRACTICES

CHAPTER 3: Move Your Body 47
CHAPTER 4: Clear Your Conscience................................ 59
CHAPTER 5: Renew Your Mind.. 79
CHAPTER 6: Refine Your Faith 105
CHAPTER 7: Process Your Emotions 131
CHAPTER 8: Center Your Heart..................................... 155
CHAPTER 9: Surrender Your Will................................. 181
CHAPTER 10: Ground Your Soul.................................... 205
CHAPTER 11: Accept Yourself 227
CHAPTER 12: Love Your Neighbor 243

ACKNOWLEDGMENTS... 279
ABOUT THE AUTHOR... 281

Introduction

"Look around this campus. If statistics are correct, most of the students will not make it through the next twenty or thirty years in ministry. Many will burn out, some will succumb to various temptations, and many will feel the stress of ministry and choose to serve as a layperson instead. This class is to teach you how to grow through trials and fulfill your call to ministry."

These were the words of the professor in one of my first seminary classes, Spiritual Formation. They sobered me, and I needed it. I thought ministry would be easy. I was wrong.

I felt all of the stressors and temptations he mentioned over the next thirty years. Those challenges triggered all my stuff—including anxiety and stress.

I had to find the peace of Jesus, or I would have been one of those statistics who did not finish the race marked out for me. This spiritual formation class inspired my lifelong passion for spiritual growth. Having Christ formed in us is the key to enduring peace.

By the grace of God, I made it through thirty years of ministry as lead pastor of two thriving churches. We learned and grew together, worshipped and served together, and rejoiced and wept together. I had to learn how to deal with my baggage, open up and be real, and connect with Jesus during hard times. Last year, the Lord called us from full-time ministry to walk alongside my wife's aging parents in Minnesota.

Not long after we arrived in Minnesota, our friend Carol called. I had not heard from her in fifteen years. She was seeking advice for her daughter Shelbi's struggle with anxiety. Shelbi grew up in our first church. I remember her as a fun-loving and big-hearted child.

As Carol talked, I was happy to hear that Shelbi was now an elementary school teacher with an active faith and a robust social life. Carol said Shelbi keeps busy all the time and that only her closest friends realize how much she struggles with anxiety.

Carol wanted to know how to help her daughter. I gave her some advice, prayed with her over the phone, and asked her to keep in touch and let me know how things were going.

After the call, I sat in silence. I felt like I hadn't done enough to help Carol or make a difference. I tried to think of a resource I could recommend that would equip Shelbi to find the peace of Christ in stressful situations.

The next day, as I continued thinking about the situation, I began writing about my battle with anxiety and how God had helped me overcome it. I also thought about people I have known who connected with Jesus in their challenging circumstances and experienced His peace. I realized that a lot of believers face similar struggles with anxiety and stress and may not be aware of how to access the peace of Christ.

That is how this book began—as a practical resource to help someone I care about but could not actually meet with for spiritual counsel and encouragement.

We all deal with various degrees of anxiety and stress. In some seasons of life, these emotions seem overwhelming.

You may be going through just such a season. These times are God-ordained moments to deepen your relationship with Him and experience the peace of Christ.

Anxiety can play an important role in our spiritual growth if we know how to make that happen. Anxiety can show us what needs to be addressed. In Scripture, Jesus met people in their anxious moments and healed them. He will do that for you.

You can have a settled spirit, a calm mind, and a confident heart in Christ. "Do not fear" is commanded, and God's peace is promised. God will deliver what He promises when we learn and take His way.

Paul wrote, "Now may the Lord of peace himself give you peace at all times and in every way. The Lord be with all of you" (II Thessalonians 3:16).

God desires to give us "peace at all times and in every way." It is His design for life. Jesus came to make that possible. He is our Good Shepherd. With Jesus, we can find tranquility by still waters and peace through the darkest valleys. The peace of Christ breaks through in our brokenness and transcends our difficult circumstances.

In our culture we have discord and strife all around us. We are more anxious than ever. The news cycle is never ending, and the commentary is never bending. Technology has advanced our social outreach but has reduced our capacity to deeply connect with one another and God.

But we take heart in this truth: the Kingdom of heaven has arrived—not in its fullness, but heaven is indeed here. Jesus taught in His first sermon, "Repent, for the kingdom of heaven has come near" (Matthew 4:17).

King Jesus has come near. He rules here and now in every willing heart and mind. Unlike selfish kings, Jesus shares everything He has with His subjects—including His peace. His reign establishes peace in all who are under His dominion.

We don't need a regime change in the world to have peace within. We just need to repent, which means have a change of mind. Under the rule of Christ, we can have blessed assurance, calm certainty, and fearless courage. We can learn to live in the peace of Jesus.

It will take practice. Anything worthwhile does. The ten practices in this book are biblical, practical, and proven. Through them God can empower you to overcome any obstacle to peace. They are at the heart of knowing God.

If we seek peace for its own sake we won't find it. But, if we seek first the kingdom of God and His righteousness, peace will be given to us (Matthew 6:33). Peace is the fruit of purposeful living according to God's plan. The ten practices taught in this book are intended to help you live out your purpose with peace in a shallow and stressful world.

You may have heard the wise saying about how to best help those in need. "You can give them a fish or teach them how to fish." What follows doesn't focus only on peaceful words, but also on proven processes that result in a deeper relationship with Jesus, our Prince of peace.

I will provide questions after each chapter to facilitate self-reflection and personal applications. These questions can also promote small group discussion if you want to invite others to take the journey with you. Consider using a journal to record your responses. These questions will help you develop habits that result in spiritual growth.

Sometimes, the practice will require a change in your focus. Some applications will call for a time commitment to balance your life in a place you probably already knew you needed some discipline. I hope these practices will give you that nudge you need and some important guidance as you begin your journey to greater purpose and peace.

In this book, I will also share how my own anxieties helped me discover and deal with the root causes of my fear. In these times of desperation, God made a way for me to access the truth and power of Jesus. When I got real with God, He worked in me.

I hope that by reading about my experiences, you will learn biblical practices that help you overcome. The Word of

God will be used throughout the book. It alone is our trust-worthy guide.

I have participated in sports all my life. When I was a lit-tle guy, I enjoyed the games but loathed the practices. But something clicked in me along the way, and I began to view practice as a way to better myself. I began to appreciate learn-ing how to get better. Then I started to enjoy training because I knew it had a purpose.

I have seen the power that even a tweak in a daily routine can make in growing closer to God and bearing fruit for His kingdom. I hope that you can learn something new and apply it to your lifestyle that will result in knowing God better. The results are godliness and peace. The work is meaningful and rewarding.

Let's begin this journey together with Jesus.

Section One

The Principles

"Do not be anxious about anything, but in every situation, by prayer and petition, with thanksgiving, present your requests to God. And the peace of God, which transcends all understanding, will guard your hearts and your minds in Christ Jesus."

- PHILIPPIANS 4:6–7

Chapter 1

Anxiety and Stress

"Therefore, do not worry about tomorrow, for tomorrow will worry about itself. Each day has enough trouble of its own."

- MATTHEW 6:34

D o you sometimes overthink a problem without seeing a solution? Does your heart race as fast as your mind over things that trigger you emotionally? If so, you know what anxiety and stress are. After looking at several different definitions of anxiety, the following is a good summary.

Anxiety: feelings of excessive fear, worry, and stress that occur about a particular event or something with an uncertain outcome.

We can experience social anxieties and separation anxieties, health and family worries, financial and work stress, phobias over public speaking, and fear of people's opinions…and I think I've experienced them all.

Anxiety and stress are a part of the general emotional classification of fear in the Bible. This general list also includes worry, panic, uneasiness, distress, and dread.

Stress can make us miserable through loss of sleep. Excessive worry will wear us down. Anxiety can keep us from engaging in normal activities like social functions or travel. We can miss out on so much that God has designed for everyone to enjoy. All of this can drain us of energy and vitality.

You Are Not the Only One

Jesus said, "In this world you will have trouble…" (John 16:33). There is not a human being alive who doesn't have trouble. The natural response to trouble is a heightened sense of stress and worry.

If these emotions persist or become excessive, they can afflict us. Stress can affect our health, strain our relationships, and limit our ability to engage in life to the fullest.

Our world does not lend itself to peaceful living. To the contrary, our culture is a media-driven, image-focused, and fast-paced society that drives us to do more, have more, know more, and be more. It's a lot of pressure to live under. But there is another way to live.

We can't let the world dictate our lives. We have to take action, be proactive, and set boundaries. Believers are to live in the world, not be of it. We must develop spiritual practices and a lifestyle that helps us stay connected to Jesus throughout our day and not get caught up by the prevailing philosophy of our world.

Still, we also have specific anxieties that have nothing to do with how our culture operates. They relate more to our own disordered thinking. It's God's plan for us to face those mountains within and overcome them through Christ. We all, like Thomas and the other disciples, have our doubts and worries. Facing them with Jesus is a normal and necessary part of our own spiritual growth.

I have heard some people say, "I have told God I will do anything for Him except fly." I usually respond by saying, "That's a good indication that God may call you to go on an international mission trip!"

It's just the way God works—to gently lead us to face our biggest fears so He can empower us to overcome them through Christ. Through that process, we will come know Jesus more powerfully, and our faith will grow.

As a pastor for thirty years, I had the privilege of sharing the spiritual journey with many people who would open up to me and confess their fears. Anxiety is a common struggle—even among those who are close to God and have walked with Him for many years. God loves us. He knows that we are sometimes troubled.

Disciples are to be learners—lifelong learners. It's a process—sometimes even a long process—but there will be defining moments along the way that will become spiritual markers of freedom from sin, worry, and anxiety.

Jesus will teach us His way of peace just like He did His disciples: "Therefore I tell you, do not worry about your life, what you will eat or drink; or about your body, what you will wear. Is not life more than food, and the body more than clothes? Look at the birds of the air; they do not sow or reap or store away in barns, and yet your heavenly Father feeds them. Are you not much more valuable than they? Can any one of you by worrying add a single hour to your life" (Matthew 6:25–26).

In these verses, Jesus is building our faith so that we will not worry or fret over our present needs or future challenges. Our Father wants His children to have confidence that He will provide for them. He promises it. We can trust Him. We are to simply grow in our faith and cooperate with His divine activity.

Self-Assessment

Where does our anxiety come from?

The following are some of the major factors that cause elevated stress and anxiety. How many of these can you relate to?

1. **Anxious thoughts** – We can't turn them off. We anticipate problems that never happen. We focus on worst-case scenarios. Questions swirl in our minds, like, *Am I going to be able to do this? Will my health hold out? Are my kids going to make it?* Worrisome thoughts about the future invade our minds almost every day.

2. **Cultural pressure** – We try hard to fit in with the people in our group. We want to be included in what they do. We feel pressure to have more possessions and to be respected, liked, successful, and accepted.

3. **Misplaced hopes** – We feel that if our leaders would just do what's right, our country would straighten up, and we wouldn't be so stressed about it. We believe if the market would be more bullish, we wouldn't worry so much. We believe if our family could just get along, then we could be at peace.

4. **Believing in lies underneath the surface** – We feel like we can't get to the bottom of what's wrong with us—like irrational fears and phobias. We wonder, *What is driving this anxiety and where does it come from?* We question ourselves and wonder why we don't have enough faith.

5. **Relational conflict** – We feel if it weren't for people, we wouldn't get so upset. We think if others would just do what they are supposed to, we could be at peace. We are sometimes still holding a grudge over how someone treated us.

6. **Difficult life events** – We haven't been able to work through a traumatic event from the past. We didn't know how to handle it when it happened, so we de-

termine to avoid thinking about it. We try to put it behind us but just can't seem to.

7. **Self-condemnation** – We are our own worst critics. We often feel like we can't do enough or be enough. We're not at peace with ourselves. We are harder on ourselves than we are on anyone else. Our instinctive response is to kick ourselves when we are down.

8. **Compartmentalizing** – We can go through a whole workday unaware that God is with us. We don't like it, but it's true. It's not that we purposely ignore God. We believe in Him, but we just forget He is there.

9. **Control issues** – We like to be in control and begin to feel stressed when we are not. Giving up control feels unsafe. We have our own ways of operating. We trust our own judgment and don't want to depend on others or ask for help. We feel anxious when we are not in control of what might happen.

10. **Fast-paced lifestyle** – We often feel hurried, and we worry about whether or not we will get everything done. We are always thinking about what needs to happen next. We like to check off our to-do list. We wish there were more hours in a day.

Were you able to see yourself in any of these descriptions? It is important to know where stress and anxiety come from because that will help you focus and grow.

The principles of peace and corresponding practices in the following chapters will equip you to overcome your fears and move forward with God.

General Anxiety and Specific Anxiety

Two types of anxiety exist: general and specific. *General* anxiety and stress come with the territory of modern life—driving to work on busy streets, working with the public, managing finances, raising kids, juggling schedules, being responsible, and the list continues.

General anxiety also includes the stress of daily living that can build up over time and weigh on us. The general angst of life in this fallen world is real. We will learn some highly effective spiritual practices to assimilate the peace of Christ in the midst of the chaos.

We also have *specific* anxieties. These are particular fears that are unrelated to our busy lifestyles. Some we may be embarrassed to admit, like the fear of heights, crowds, water, or even death. It seems like everyone has at least one trigger point that causes panic, from the thought of public speaking to the fear of being called on to read by the class teacher, etc.

Our specific anxieties can also stem from a big life event like divorce, loss of a job or loved one, trauma, abuse, a cancer diagnosis...these particular events can make us susceptible to anxiety and panic attacks that we never experienced before. I'll address how to deal with those as well.

The enemy knows when we are at our weakest, and he always takes that opportunity to make us miserable. These particular anxieties can be overcome with the gracious help of the Holy Spirit.

I will share testimonies of specific anxieties with which I struggled and tell you how I found peace. They may not be the same as your specific anxiety, but the pathway to overcome them will be similar. When victory comes over a *specific* anxiety, there will be no struggle, no maintenance required, no more nervousness when triggered—just peace and calm. Some internal work must be done to get there, and it may require several attempts; but if you persevere in them, then you can find victory too.

Self-Help Strategies

Our world offers many self-help strategies for peace like spa visits, more vacations, breathing exercises…and there is nothing wrong with these things. I like vacations. But they fall short of the true peace Jesus offers His followers because they don't address the deeper issues of truth and grace, meaning and purpose…. We need God's help to adopt these peacemaking values in our lives.

Another ineffective coping strategy we sometimes employ is the avoidance of triggers—the things that set off our fears. We tend to avoid the situations with which we don't feel comfortable, but those are the very situations God may want us to be in to fulfill His purposes. If He wills that we enter into those places that cause us stress, He will give us a pathway to find His peace.

I heard someone say, "The poison is part of the cure." Facing our fears is an important part of growing in Christ. He could use that challenge to reveal what's wrong in us, change it, and make us more like Jesus. It's a work of God.

We will address how to regularly position ourselves to experience this work of God. It's a normal part of spiritual growth.

The mere absence of conflict is not peace. The peace taught in Scripture speaks of a living peace given by the Living God. God's peace is a deep pleasure and inner tranquility that transcends any challenging situation. Horatio Spafford's hymn, "It Is Well with My Soul," says it so well in the first stanza and chorus:

When peace like a river attendeth my way,
When sorrows like sea billows roll,
Whatever my lot, Thou hast taught me to say,
It is well, it is well with my soul.

It is well (it is well)
With my soul (with my soul).
It is well, it is well with my soul.

A False Peace

Our world has a "me-centered" philosophy that promises peace through doing what seems right to the individual. "Me" has usurped God's rightful place. This worldview calls evil good and good evil.

It promises peace through what "seems right to a man," but that philosophy actually causes stress and anxiety. We were never meant to live through our own understanding, but by faith in God's Spirit-inspired Word.

This humanistic philosophy is bringing more and more tension and strife through self-assertion and willful demands—which are not at all in line with the cross of Jesus Christ. It basically says we can do it all ourselves, our way and any way.

God spoke through the prophet Ezekiel about the false prophets in his day who gave people false hope: "Because they lead my people astray, saying, 'Peace,' when there is no peace, and because, when a flimsy wall is built, they cover it with whitewash" (Ezekiel 13:10).

This whitewashed wall looks great on the outside, but underneath the whitewash, the wall is flimsy and unable to offer protection. Beware of the false peace the world offers. It may seem good, but it won't deliver real and lasting security.

We know that when we have the peace of Christ, that peace will hold true in the heat of battle. It does not depend on what men say or do. It's sourced in Jesus and the Word of God, not in the minds of men.

"'There is no peace,' says the LORD, 'for the wicked'" (Isaiah 48:22).

The wicked do not trust or obey God, therefore, they will not have deep or lasting peace. We have lived under this cultural influence and have been conditioned by it more than we realize. It is based on a materialistic, man-centered worldview that has seeped into our way of viewing life.

Violating God's design for family, relationships, or morality will only bring discord and distress. Obedience to Jesus will change our self-focused worldview and instill in us the virtues and ideals of heaven. Pure and wholesome thoughts result from the gospel way of living in purity and love.

Pride and vanity are high on the list of worldly ideals. They falsely promise the elevation of the self. The person that remains influenced by this mindset will not have peace. Our soul was never intended to live like this. It's stressful to keep up an image—and get people to buy into that image. It's a never-ending cycle.

Resting in Christ restores your soul. Let Jesus minister to you before you minister for Him. When we rest in His grace, God restores us in peace. Somewhere, sometime in your day, let go and unwind in Jesus. Let your weary soul be unburdened in Christ. Then you can follow Him in paths of righteousness, empowered to do His will.

From Self-Talk to Quiet Trust

The phrase "fear not" is used in the Bible 365 times. I smile when I think about how many days per year we are faced with challenges that will at least tempt us to fear. When we give in to fear, our mind spins like a top to find a solution. We all talk to ourselves. Self-talk is a coping mechanism from a mind that perceives threats of every kind and is unaware of the Help beside us. If there are no perceived threats, our mind will invent them and mentally rehearse how to cope.

The ceaseless chatter within our heads causes much anxiety and stress. People try to find ways to calm their mind and relax. But, sooner or later, stressful thoughts return. A mind always on alert seeks to identify threats and control them. But there is a better way to live that quiets the soul.

God has designed us to operate on trust. Fear is a sign that something is wrong in us, a symptom of the lack of trust in Jesus and His truth. In coming chapters, we will cover how to use that fear to locate the source of a particular anxiety and cooperate with Jesus to remove it.

As with physical pain, we must stop trying to remedy our anxiety by ourselves and go to our Great Physician. It's a big first step of faith to say, "I am powerless to help myself. I can't even control my own thoughts. I need a Physician."

Then we act on that belief and go to Jesus, our Physician. He will want us to show Him where the pain is coming from, where it is located. Then He will give us a diagnosis and a remedy.

With Jesus, the remedy is almost always the revelation of His love and His real presence in our lives. In the coming chapters, I will outline how to visit with the Great Physician in prayer to get the help we need.

If we leave our fear untreated, it will sabotage our decision making and cause us to shrink back. But we can use fear to help us locate the part of us that is not operating from faith. We will need to search our hearts, then the Holy Spirit can help us apply the truth there to be free.

The peaceful way of Jesus comes from spiritual growth grounded in God's Word and produced by God's Spirit. Jesus is not rude, forceful, or aggressive. But He is very compelling and powerful, good to all who come to Him for help.

I am not a professional counselor, and I offer no medical or psychological advice. I approach this topic from a spiritual point of view, which includes our whole person. It's a biblical approach to life's challenges.

In the next chapter, you will learn the biblical principles of peace. These powerful truths can be experienced in the heart of every believer. It takes practice. But the practices covered in chapters three through twelve produce the life-giving fruit of the Spirit that will fill every area of your life with God's goodness.

Questions for Reflection and Application

(Consider using a journal to record your responses to the application questions.)

1. Focus on what makes you anxious then define anxiety in your own words.

2. In the "Self-Assessment" section, which statements could you identify with the most? Describe your struggle.

3. What self-help strategies have you tried that haven't worked very well for you?

4. What are the differences between the peace the world strives to achieve and the peace God offers?

5. "Come to me, all you who are weary and burdened, and I will give you rest" (Matthew 11:28).

   a. Are you weary from stress and burdened with worry? If so, what causes it and how does it make you feel?

   b. What does Jesus mean when He says, "I will give you rest"?

6. Write a prayer asking God for help as you take this journey to know the peace of Christ.

Chapter 2

The Principles of Peace

*"Peace I leave with you; my peace I give you. I do not
give to you as the world gives. Do not let your hearts be
troubled and do not be afraid."*

- JOHN 14:27

W e must have a biblical foundation for every endeavor.
Finding peace is no exception. The enemy promises
peace through the ways of the world. These ways appeal to
our natural understanding. They seem like a way to peace but
lead in the opposite direction—to a short-lived, self-focused
counterfeit. Only God promises real and lasting peace. And
He delivers!

The seven principles that follow form the biblical foundation of peace.

Principle #1 – Peace Follows Purpose

Peace is not a one-and-done transaction. Peace is the fruit of
a lifestyle that connects us with God's ultimate purpose.

What are we here on earth for? In a sentence, we exist to
glorify God by becoming like Jesus. We were created to be

like God. It's the "new you" Paul described in Ephesians 4, "put on the new self, created to be like God, in true righteousness and holiness" (v.26).

It's the loftiest purpose ever known—to partake of God's divine nature, to reflect His likeness as dearly loved children, and to share His eternal mission. Peace is imbedded in our purpose and our new identity.

God works in us to that end—to form Christ in us for the glory of His name. God moves powerfully in every circumstance of life to remake us in His own image—holy and loving.

Paul wrote an important verse in Romans 8 that links God's ultimate purpose to His premiere promise to us: "And we know that in all things God works for the good of those who love him, who have been called according to his purpose. For those God foreknew he also predestined to be conformed to the image of his Son, that he might be the firstborn among many brothers and sisters" (Romans 8:28–29).

We have been predestined to be conformed to the image of Jesus. God's purpose for your life connects you to God's work in every season of life—even the hardest seasons. God forms His character in us during those times.

Paul wrote, "Not only so, but we also glory in our sufferings, because we know that suffering produces perseverance; perseverance, character; and character, hope" (Romans 5:3–4). Peace and hope flow from godly character—love, faithfulness, honesty. God forms His character in us over time as we persevere in doing His will.

Have you settled on your ultimate purpose—to glorify God by becoming more like Jesus? Embrace Jesus as your life, and you will find meaning in everything—from celebrating to suffering. Peace in everything is promised because God's at work in all things to bring about our highest good—to become like Jesus for the glory of His name.

When we get our purpose right, peace will emerge in every trial. The nature of Christ is peace. When we become more like Him, we have more peace.

Paul wrote from jail, "For to me to live is Christ and to die is gain" (Philippians 1:21). He could have allowed his present circumstances to dictate how he felt. Instead, he experienced God at work in his hardship to glorify His name.

Self-concern had evaporated in Paul with the knowledge that Christ had taken hold of his life to accomplish His purpose. Whether in jail or not, Paul focused on doing what he was supposed to be doing each moment and leaving the outcomes to God.

Paul's heart was guarded in jail by the peace of Christ, not a Roman soldier.

Principle #2 – Harmony with God

The peace of Christ comes from living in harmony with God and His will. When mind and will are aligned with God, then we move with Him and share His peace. The peace of Christ is not the absence of outward chaos or challenge, but the inner tranquility that results from our union with God in Christ. It's an unshakeable peace that gives birth to courage in daily living.

Spiritual harmony results from believing in God's Word and then acting in God's will. Mary said to the angel, "I am the Lord's servant, may your word to me be fulfilled" (Luke 1:38). Paul writes, "Paul, called to be an apostle of Christ Jesus by the will of God" (I Corinthians 1:1).

We all have a calling to carry out, gifts to employ, duties to fulfill, and commandments to follow all according to the will of God. It's God's design for our life. And we are to accomplish His will though Christ who gives us strength and peace. He works powerfully in us to accomplish His will.

In an orchestra, when all the instruments are played in harmony with the written music and the timing of the director, beautiful symphonies are produced. But all it takes is just one note to be played off key or the timing to be off a fraction of a second, then dissonance occurs.

Dissonance is tension or a clash of musical notes. It's not pleasant when that happens. If it lasts for very long, the listener suffers and wants relief. That describes anxiety and stress—when mind, will, or actions are not in unison with God's will. Discord happens in us when we aren't in sync with God.

If we bring our whole life under the direction of Jesus, a soul-satisfying peace will result. Christ's peace is an inner calm and quiet assurance that allows us to live in the present with confidence and look into the future with a smile.

All of us have the same general musical score as revealed in the Word of God. We are to play those notes together with other like-minded believers. But each of us will also have unique parts.

You have important assignments in God's redemptive plan. Know your assignments. Each of us will have unique callings to complete, duties to fulfill, sacrifices to make, and people to love according to God's will. Be at peace with your part.

Let go of the pressure of trying to be like someone else. We can't be at peace playing someone else's music. Just be who you are in Christ and live for the applause of One. You are dearly loved and divinely chosen to serve the Lord according to His Word and His will.

Eric Liddell was the son of missionary parents to China in the early in 1920s. He, too, felt called to serve there. When Eric left China to attend college in his native Scotland, he excelled in sports, especially running. After college, he was considering running in the 1924 Olympic Games in Paris.

But his sister, Mary, pressed him to remember his call to missionary service in China and prepare to go back. He agreed with her about his call, but he also had a conviction that he was to run in the Olympics. In the movie *Chariots of Fire*, he replied to her, "I believe God made me for a purpose, but he also made me fast. And when I run I feel His pleasure."

Liddell went on to compete in the 1924 summer Olympic Games, winning the gold medal in the 400-meter race. Afterwards, he continued serving Christ as a missionary in China.

When we do what God has called us to do, then we experience God's pleasure and peace in our hearts. Every calling has challenges, hardships, and tests. Mary had hers, Paul had his, and Eric Liddell had his own. But through them all, God worked to bring about His purpose and His plan. He will do the same for you.

Principle #3 – Jesus Is Our Peace

Peace is found in a Person. When you become anxious or afraid, go to Jesus. He is your refuge. You can rest in Him. He is your safe place. Jesus promises His peace to everyone who goes through turmoil.

Jesus gave the disciples this very promise before they entered a season of chaos. He said: "A time is coming and in fact has come when you will be scattered, each to your own home. You will leave me all alone. Yet I am not alone, for my Father is with me. I have told you these things, so that in me you may have peace. In this world you will have trouble. But take heart! I have overcome the world" (John 16:32-33).

Jesus is preparing His disciples for the trouble and persecution awaiting them as they do His will. But He says, "In me you may have peace...I have overcome the world."

Trouble is natural but peace is supernatural. That's why peace in Jesus cannot be shaken by any natural threat because He is over nature. He has overcome, and He instills in you this assurance—through Jesus you, too, will overcome. Jesus is your victory.

This peace will guard your heart as you do His will. When you realize this truth and experience it, then nothing but peace can abide in you. You know everything is going to be all right no matter what may come.

C.S. Lewis wrote, "God cannot give us a happiness and peace apart from Himself, because it is not there. There is no such thing."[1]

How do you know you have the peace of Jesus? When there is chaos on the outside of you and peace on the inside— then you know that peace didn't come from the world or even yourself. That peace came from abiding in Jesus.

God wants you to live from there. Jesus is the sanctuary where we meet with God. Sin took peace far from us, but God sent His Son to restore it to everyone who would believe.

---

[1] C.S. Lewis, *Mere Christianity,* (New York: Macmillan, 1952), 53-54.

"But he was pierced for our transgressions, he was crushed for our iniquities; the punishment that brought us peace was on him, and by his wounds we are healed" (Isaiah 53:5).

True and everlasting peace is not earned, it's given. It's a gift of His grace to all who turn to Him in repentance and faith. Trusting Jesus brings us peace with God. Believers can know peace on earth because God's gracious favor shines on them.

Jesus doesn't want our hearts to be troubled. He wants us to have His peace. "For to us a child is born, to us a son is given and the government will be on his shoulders. And he will be called Wonderful Counselor, Mighty God, Everlasting Father, Prince of Peace" (Isaiah 9:6).

When the government of my life is on the shoulders of Jesus, my mind is at rest. When I take control, it's as if everything is all on me. That's the definition of stress.

When I lean on my own understanding, I worry about my life. Will I have enough? What will people think? Am I going to make it? And on and on the doubts and worries go.

The peace of Christ is not "as the world gives." Therefore, we must *unlearn* some of the coping strategies of the world to *unwrap* the gift of peace in Jesus. He loves us and gives Himself to all who put their trust in Him. Jesus, not our striving, gives us peace.

Principle #4 – A Renewed Mind

We were created to live in truth. Our minds were once in harmony with the eternal Word of God. But, mankind fell from God because we trusted in the enemy's lies rather than God's truth. That's the origin of stress and anxiety. Our natural mind has fallen into its own anxious thoughts.

God is not in our fearful thoughts. That's why we must not be guided by them. They will lead us down a worrisome road.

God is in His Word. Our mind needs to be renewed in the Word of God. His Word gives light for our path and the knowledge of God's abiding presence.

Our mind can be renewed because God acts to form His mind in us. He accomplishes that work by His Spirit through His Word as we read, pray, and make application. He puts His Word in our heart and writes it on our mind (Hebrews 10:16). When we live with the mind of Christ, our constant self-chatter settles down and gives way to a calm assurance.

The gospel has the mindset we need. Thoughts of faith, hope, and love are imbedded in this good news. We are to live with these thoughts of Jesus that are filled with grace and peace toward us.

The Word reveals that God is in control. He has a plan. The plan will come about. There is a season for everything. Nothing that sets itself up against His plan will prosper. We have nothing to fear.

He is for us not against us. Knowing in your heart that you have the gift of His favor, love, and sovereignty over your life will carry you through any hard time with peace of mind.

The American mindset never rests. We want more information, more entertainment, more stimulation…The devil distracts us and captivates us with a constant stream of images and messages. Our natural mind has been corrupted. If we live in our thoughts, we will be distressed.

Practices to renew our mind are on God's agenda for every believer. They are highly effective. We have been given a precious gift in God's Word. Practice will help us assimilate this powerful Word into our mind.

Principle #5 – Faith Overcomes Fear

The promised peace of God is conditioned on one thing—believing in Jesus. So, this is our great work in overcoming anxiety—trusting in Jesus. He teaches His followers to live by faith. Faith in Jesus will keep us calm in the storms of life.

Jesus was sleeping in a boat on a stormy sea but was roused up by His frightened and frantic disciples. "He replied, 'You of little faith, why are you so afraid?' Then he got up and rebuked the winds and the waves, and it was completely calm. The men were amazed and asked, 'What kind of man is this? Even the winds and the waves obey him!'" (Matthew 8:26–27).

Jesus didn't cut the disciples any slack about their fear or lack of faith. But He did help their faith to form by allowing them to see what He did. He rebuked the wind and the waves and calmed them, showing His disciples that He rules over all creation.

God reveals Himself to us through His Word in our trials. The Holy Spirit will make Jesus real to us in the midst of our storms so we, too, can believe.

The disciples asked the right question: "What kind of man is this?" He is more than a teacher. He is God over everything—including nature. That's why trusting in Him results in peace.

When Jesus first broke the news to His disciples that He would be leaving them after three years together, He said, "Do not let your hearts be troubled. You believe in God; believe also in me" (John 14:1).

Our faith is not just a leap in the dark. It is not blind. It's not wishful thinking or man's imagination to deal with despair. No, our minds have been enlightened. Our hearts have been illuminated by the Holy Spirit and the Word of God. God discloses Himself to us so that we may believe in the Truth. We don't have to try to figure it out or strive to understand it on our own.

We see and perceive the greatest things through faith. That's why our peace is stronger than any situation we face. Faith overcomes anything that meets the human eye because God and His divine revelation are stronger than anything we can see.

King David described this unshakeable peace when he wrote, "Even though I walk through the darkest valley, I will fear no evil, for you are with me; your rod and your staff, they comfort me" (Psalm 23:4).

The spiritual truth that God was with him carried the day and carried David in undefeatable confidence through the darkest valley. God's Holy Spirit enlightened David to the spiritual fact that God was with him. And God had a rod in His hand to vanquish any enemy. He had a staff in His other hand, revealing to David that he could trust God's wisdom and guidance.

Our faith is based on spiritual facts of real substance. These facts are the most powerful, eternal realities known in the universe. When believers perceive the truth, victory over fear prevails.

Spiritual truths are supernatural. Any natural threat seen through the eyes of faith ceases to hold any sway. It's no longer perceived as a threat. God is greater. God's Word is eternal, unshakeable, and undiminished by the world no matter what men may say.

Over the years in ministry, I have encountered people of faith who have faced uncertainty, strife, and all manner of trials. Many reported that they had peace knowing their situation was in God's hands, and they knew they were going to be okay no matter what happened.

Most of them did not have that peace initially, but by the working of the Holy Spirit in the trial, faith was formed and assurance came.

We, too, will come upon mountains that seemingly can't be moved, Goliaths that give us a panic attack, or Red Seas that look impassable. If that is the case for you right now, anxiety is often our initial and natural response to what is perceived as a threat to us.

But God will not want us to remain in that fear very long. He will shepherd us like He did David to know the spiritual power—how close He is and how safe we are with Him who is over all.

Faith sets us free from worry and gives us confidence. Faith breeds conviction and courage to "fight the good fight, keep the faith, and finish the course marked out for us" (II Timothy 4:7).

Faith is not naive. Faith faces facts like death and says, "'Where, O death, is your victory? Where, O death, is your sting?' The sting of death is sin, and the power of sin is the law. But thanks be to God! He gives us the victory through our Lord Jesus Christ" (I Corinthians 15:55–57).

That is the kind of faith God wants us to have when we face our fears.

Principle #6 – The Holy Spirit

Peace is the fruit of knowing God and living by His Spirit. Paul writes of the wonderful, soul-satisfying fruit: "So I say, walk by the Spirit, and you will not gratify the desires of the flesh...But the fruit of the Spirit is love, joy, peace, forbearance, kindness, goodness, faithfulness, gentleness and self-control. Against such things there is no law" (Galatians 5:16, 22-23).

No law can take away the fruit of the Spirit. No person can steal your peace when it's sourced in God. Not even Satan. If we don't believe what the enemy says, then the lies he assaults us with cannot take our peace. Jesus is greater, truth is stronger, and love is more powerful than any devil.

Over time, the Holy Spirit will help you to know the truth and the peace that comes from Christ who said to His disciples: "But the Advocate, the Holy Spirit, whom the Father will send in my name, will teach you all things and will remind you of everything I have said to you. Peace I leave with you; my peace I give you. I do not give to you as the world gives. Do not let your hearts be troubled and do not be afraid" (John 14:26–27).

Holy Spirit-inspired truth will demolish the strongholds of the enemy's lies embedded in our internal belief system. The lies bring anxiety and unrest.

We may have experienced those lies years ago, prior to conversion. Your experiences may have produced a view of reality that doesn't include unconditional love or the super-natural understanding of God's presence. We can learn spiritual, peace-producing truths from the Holy Spirit.

David wrote, "…you know me. You know when I sit and when I rise; you perceive my thoughts from afar. You discern my going out and my lying down. You are familiar with all my ways" (Psalm 139:1–3).

God knows you, too. He formed you and loves you. He sent His Spirit to be your Counselor. And your Counselor is wonderful. He will help you and show you the way that leads to peace. He will be working in you as you engage in proven practices that produce a peaceful lifestyle.

Principle #7 – Effective Practices

We don't grow in our relationship with Jesus only by having a goal. We will go as far as our practice takes us.

Spiritual practices are intentional daily habits that form a routine of life. This routine becomes a lifestyle that forms Christ in us. These habits keep us mindful of God's presence, aligned with His will, and alive in His Spirit. It's a lifestyle of peace grounded in God's love. It is the perfect soil to grow every good fruit—even in hard times.

Will Durant wrote, "We are what we repeatedly do. Excellence, then, is not an act, but a habit."[2] The right daily habits will form Christ and His peace in every believer. You will become what you repeatedly do.

It takes discipline, but once you get in a routine, you begin to love the lifestyle because it anchors your life in Jesus.

Spiritual practices are really just our participation in God's action to restore His image and likeness in us. Theologians call this process *sanctification*. It's God's work in every believer.

Our specific callings will be different—where we live and work, whether we are married or single, whether we are young or old—but our goal in all things will be the same: to glorify God by becoming like Jesus. As we more intentionally live purpose-driven lives, our peace will grow, and we will become less apt to be shaken.

Jesus had regular disciplines and customs. He sought God's will every day, surrendered to Him every moment, did what He saw the Father doing, and followed Him where He led. He read God's Word. He listened to His voice. He retreated to lonely places. He arose while it was still dark to meet with God. He sensed God at work around Him all the time (John 5:17) and joined Him.

---

[2] The Nicomachean Ethics, Book II, 4; Book I, 7, as quoted by Will Durant *The Story of Philosophy*, (New York, NY: Simon and Schuster, 1926), *no page number available.*

Jesus did not fret over the future but stayed in the moment as He walked with God and served people. It's the simplified life—and it's profoundly peaceful. It's living by the Spirit in the here and now without our mind racing forward or getting stuck in the past. God's design is for us to live with Him, listen to Him, and do His will.

I read a book as a young minister about how to have a healthy long-term ministry. The chapter on marriage taught pastors and their wives to date weekly, depart quarterly, and vacation annually. That stuck with me. I took it to heart.

I practiced this routine for thirty-two years almost without fail. It served me well. Without that discipline, I could have easily drifted, becoming unbalanced in my priorities and unfruitful in my marriage. I could have lost it all.

Instead, my wife Dana and I grew together as we took care of our relationship. We have simple habits and routines in our marriage that we both enjoy very much. I love our rhythm of life.

The same is true with my relationship with God. I have daily routines and habits I look forward to because they bring me such joy and peace. That wasn't always the case.

For instance, I used to struggle with quiet times. I didn't feel like I connected with God much in prayer. I kept at it though because I knew it was one of the undeniable keys to growth.

Perseverance is an important part of the equation in every spiritual practice. There is a learning curve.

Also, the other practices I undertook, like Bible reading, started to positively influence my prayer life. The practices are interrelated. They feed off of each other. Over time, these habits foster a fruit-bearing relationship with Jesus.

Our goal will be fully realized when Jesus returns. We will see Him in all of His glory coming for us. And we will be changed—even glorified as we behold Jesus face to face. This will complete the transformation to His likeness.

We will live with God forever as His children and share in His awesome kingdom. Until then we are in the process of sharing in the nature of Jesus. Peace is His nature. We share in His peace.

Spiritual practices don't result from emotional decisions that depend on willpower. The decision has to come from a settled belief that I want to be like Jesus more than anything else. God wills it for me. Spiritual practices are the pathway to fulfill my purpose and God's plan.

Many of these habits don't take any more of your time—just more focus and intention. It takes a willingness to orient your life to becoming more like Jesus, to partake of His divine nature and share in His eternal mission.

Commit your life to having Christ formed in you to the glory of God. These practices and others like them will help you on this lifelong journey.

Then you just say to yourself, "When I fall, I am going to get up. When I have a bad day, I'm still going to do practice. If I fail, I'm going to get back on track. It's going to take time, but I am going to live more in harmony with Jesus and with the conscious awareness of God's Presence."

It's a great journey with God. On this journey, you will discover more love than you ever imagined and more peace than you ever thought possible.

Acquiring peace is a lifestyle of faith, not an event. The following practices will help you develop your spiritual life and experience the peace of Christ.

Questions for Reflection and Application

1. Do you agree or disagree with the statement, "Our ultimate goal and purpose in life is to glorify God by becoming like Jesus."

    a. Have you embraced God's ultimate purpose for your life?

    b. Write out a prayer committing or recommitting your life to your ultimate purpose.

2. Peace comes when we are in harmony with God. When our mind and will are aligned with His, then we are blessed with divine peace. Why is that so?

    a. Recall a time in your life when you felt you were walking in harmony with God. What spiritual practices were helping you align with God's will?

    b. Describe a time when you felt pressure to be like another person who seems to be doing so much for God. How did that make you feel?

    c. Do you feel anxiety now because you don't feel good enough? Write out a prayer confessing this pressure and letting it go to Jesus. Afterwards, take time to listen to what Jesus may be saying to you in response.

3. We don't become like Jesus by simply having a goal. We will go as far as our practice takes us. Our spiritual prac-

tices are our participation in God's work to form Christ in us. They enable us to reach our goal.

a. Think of an important goal you have achieved—in school, sports, health, career, family, etc. What regular practices did you employ to enable you to reach that goal?

b. Write down the practices that were most difficult to maintain and why they were so crucial to achieving your goal?

4. "Spiritual practices don't result from emotional decisions that depend on our willpower. The decision has to come from a settled belief that I want to be like Jesus more than anything else." How do you feel about that statement?

a. Recall an emotional decision you made that didn't last long. What do emotional commitments lack?

b. What are necessary elements when it comes to making decisions that result in forming habits that become a routine and a lifestyle?

Section Two

The Practices

"Whatever you have learned or received or heard from me, or seen in me—put it into practice. And the God of peace will be with you."

- PHILIPPIANS 4:9

Chapter 3

Move Your Body

*"The LORD God took the man and put him in the
Garden of Eden to work it and take care of it."*

- GENESIS 2:15

We were made to move. Move with God and enjoy creation. This activity promotes health and a sense of well-being for a reason—it's God's design. Stress is relieved and peace flows when we are living according to this design.

It was the custom of Adam and Eve to walk with God "in the cool of the day" (Genesis 3:8). Maybe it was after their work in the garden—maybe before. We know it was in the cool of the day. It's a custom that needs to be recaptured today. God intends for us to move in creation and allow the experience to refresh us.

Let's look at how we were created: "Then the LORD God formed a man from the dust of the ground and breathed into his nostrils the breath of life, and the man became a living being" (Genesis 2:7). We come from the dust. We also come from God. We are a "living being" or soul—we are body, mind, and spirit, yet one person.

All three parts of us are interrelated. Physicians tell us there is a definite connection between our physical, emotional, and mental well-being. There is an even more profound connection with our spiritual health.

We will be less susceptible to stress and anxiety when we tend to all the components of the human soul. That's why I begin with the physical component.

Even Christian monks who have devoted their lives to a spiritual life of prayer work hard five or six days a week at mostly manual labor. Why? They say work makes their prayer lives stronger.

We must pay attention to each aspect of our being to live a lifestyle of peace. Each one impacts the other.

Let Creation Renew You

If you don't get outside, you will live in your head, get stuck in your small world, and be oppressed by petty problems.

We need to smell the fresh air, let the breeze flow across our faces, and take in the God-designed beauty all around us. There are animals to watch and flowers to appreciate. We need to the feel the sun, see the stars, and listen to the water flowing.

The purpose of God's creation is more than provision. It's beautiful, refreshing, renewing, and to be enjoyed with God.

Adam and Eve personally named the animals, worked the garden, and communed with God in this place. While creation now groans for its redemption, it continues to exist for us, for our well-being. In the end, the leaves of the trees will be for the healing of the nations.

John wrote, "Then the angel showed me the river of the water of life, as clear as crystal, flowing from the throne of God and of the Lamb down the middle of the great street of the city. On each side of the river stood the tree of life, bearing twelve crops of fruit, yielding its fruit every month. And the leaves of the tree are for the healing of the nations" (Revelation 22:1–2).

This future scene of a glorious river, beautiful trees, and its crops of fruit serve the grand purpose of healing and renewal. Creation today plays a similar role in our own healing and renewal. Not getting outside on a regular basis is like having a house with no windows. It isn't healthy.

Creation is our Father's world made for His children to live in and enjoy. Creation is a spiritual pathway to experience God in a setting intended for this. Its Architect and Builder sought out fellowship with His children in the midst of the garden He created and Adam and Eve tended. Practice soul care by making time to connect with Him there.

Creation speaks. We need to listen. It declares the glory of God. That's why creation can renew our mind and calm our nerves as we take in its important message.

"The heavens declare the glory of God; the skies proclaim the work of his hands. Day after day they pour forth speech; night after night they reveal knowledge. They have no speech, they use no words; no sound is heard from them. Yet their voice goes out into all the earth, their words to the ends of the world" (Psalm 19:1–4). Let their voice be heard.

Stop and notice the colors, observe the clouds, and listen to the birds. What are these things saying to you about God? Let them speak to you.

The sky gives us perspective. The animals give us joy and remind us of God's goodness and provision. We remember His eye is on the sparrow, and we are worth more. The sun rises in the morning proclaiming God's faithfulness. The heavens declare His glory and eternal power. They reveal knowledge of God. Through our interaction with creation, our spirit is refreshed.

Made to Move

The human body has 360 joints. They were made to move. I heard a physical therapist say to a patient once, "The life of a joint is movement." If we don't move the joint, it can lose its range of motion or become weak and susceptible to injury. If we don't move our body, our mind will suffer.

Often, we can combine exercise with getting outdoors. Except for lightning or really bad conditions, don't let the weather rule you. You can put on the right clothes and get out in just about any weather to take a walk. You might be surprised by what you enjoy.

My favorite weather to run in is a light rain or fresh snow. Be careful. Don't be reckless. Practice safety. You may have physical limitations. That's okay. Just get out there when possible and experience the elements. And enjoy your walk with God. If getting outside isn't an option, get moving somewhere—a gym, a mall, a home workout room....

I get out and exercise just as much for my mental and spiritual health as for my physical health. It reboots my energy. I have more mental clarity. What seemed so big and stressful to me before exercising doesn't seem so big afterwards.

After a long day at work, the last thing my flesh wants to do is exercise. I am exhausted and tired. But I discovered a few years ago that most of my tiredness came from mental and emotional exertion.

I sat most of the day studying, counseling, or planning. When I visited people, I drove and then usually sat or stood. But at the end of a typical workday, I often felt worn out. All I wanted to do was recline. My flesh always talked to me and said, "Sit down and relax! You need to rest."

Whether it was when I got home from work in the evening or when I got out of bed in the morning, I had to overcome this tired sluggishness to get out the door to exercise. At those times, the only thing that got me out the door was an already decided conviction that I was going to do this. It affected everything I did in a positive way.

This got me out the door, and soon, the blood got flowing, my mind started clearing, and those endorphins started doing what God created them to do. By the end, I felt great—

not tired at all. It wasn't my body that needed to rest. My body needed to move, and when it did, my mind was cleared, and my negative emotions were released.

It's a spiritual practice God intended to practice with us. So, "in the cool of the day," walk with God in the garden He created.

Be Like a Kid

"But Jesus said, 'Let the little children come to me, and do not hinder them! For the kingdom of heaven belongs to such as these'" (Matthew 19:14).

Kids move and have a lot of fun doing it. They know how to cut loose and enjoy being outside. We need to take a page out of their playbook for happiness and apply it to this practice. And aren't we supposed to be like a kid in some ways as Christians?

Laughter is like a medicine. If we always take ourselves too seriously, we will miss out on some lighter moments intended to lighten our way. Exercise can be a lot of fun if we just let ourselves go and enjoy it.

It's not just about getting it done so we can check it off our "to do" list. I think that is why Dana always says to me when I go out the door to exercise, "Enjoy!"

Riding a bicycle makes me feel like a kid again out on an adventure. I hop on my hybrid bike in the garage and hit the dedicated bike trail just a short distance away. I enjoy the view, the wind, the light, and the scenery. I like picking up speed going downhill and feeling the burn pedaling up.

My favorite all-time exercise was meeting at the YMCA with friends before work twice a week to play pick-up basketball. We were politely competitive and had good fellowship. I looked forward to those times and always left ready to engage the responsibilities of the day. I felt like a kid playing ball with my buddies.

Guys like recreational companionship. We need to have an excuse to have good fellowship and develop friendships. Basketball wasn't outside, but it was alongside the pinnacle of God's creation that bears His blessed image. A good bunch of guys, redeemed by the Lord, can bless your soul as you move together in good-natured fun and games.

Find What Works for You

God will guide you to discover what you enjoy doing. Try something new. Maybe you don't necessarily like working out, but with the right friend you could enjoy fishing, kayaking, or walking at church. Ever tried pickle ball?

Our family enjoyed gardening together for years. One of my new friends here in Minnesota asked, "Do you have a pair of snowshoes? They are great for hiking up here in the winter, you know."

Convenience is essential to repeat the practice. Maybe a gym on the way to work or a park nearby will make it easy for you to incorporate exercise into your lifestyle. On the weekends, a trip to a favorite hiking or walking trail might be a good option. Hiking through the woods and alongside creeks can take you away mentally and recharge your batteries.

Everything from our immune system to our mental clarity will benefit from moving with God in His creation.

Some people get plenty of exercise at work—maybe even 7,000 steps. They need rest! Some work outside. I was inside with people all day or studying, so I needed to break out into creation and move with God.

It's biblical, but we need balance. Paul wrote the following verse that puts it in perspective. "For physical training is of some value, but godliness has value for all things, holding promise for both the present life and the life to come" (I Timothy 4:8).

The Romans worked out for vanity's sake. We aren't trying to sculpt something for people to envy. It's okay to want to look good and feel good. Just keep it in perspective. The core reason is to live more according to the plan God intended.

Disconnecting from our man-made environment and moving with God in creation renews our souls. If you can't be outside, exercise inside and later look out your window or sit on your porch for a few minutes and look up into the sky. Take it all in. Notice the beauty.

Don't overdo it, but don't neglect it either. We need around thirty to forty-five minutes of exercise on most days. Balance is the key.

Don't let being outside or engaging in exercise become a burden. You will learn to enjoy what God has given you to do and enjoy His fellowship along the way. A little care for your body promises to make each aspect of your life better. Let's rediscover the rhythm of life with God that He intends for us to enjoy.

The Fall and Hope of Restoration

In a very important scene in the Garden of Eden, we see this: "Then the man and his wife heard the sound of the LORD God as he was walking in the garden in the cool of the day, and they hid from the LORD God among the trees of the garden. But the LORD God called to the man, 'Where are you?' He answered, 'I heard you in the garden, and I was afraid because I was naked; so I hid'" (Genesis 3:8–10).

We live in a fallen world. In the above verse, God was walking in the garden, but Adam and Eve were afraid. They hid from God because of their shame.

The same kind of fear pervades our world because of this same estrangement from God. This is where stress comes from. Insecurities masked by innumerable coping mechanisms are everywhere—diversions, escapes, distractions.

Believers who have been reconciled and have peace with God through Jesus are still influenced by the fallen world. Our culture, its mentality, and worldview are a part of us—especially our stress level.

The next nine practices cover mental, spiritual, and relational aspects of our restoration in Christ. I won't be describing physical movements like I did in this chapter. But there are spiritual movements, internal transactions, and mental adjustments to make that will empower you to be like Jesus and overcome stress and anxiety.

Questions for Reflection and Application

1. How do you experience God outside in creation? What speaks to you?

2. How have you released stress through exercise or physical labor?

3. List some activities you enjoyed outside as a child. Is there a way you could recapture some of those light-hearted moments in outdoor activities?

4. For exercise to become a lifelong habit, it must be convenient. What are some ways you could fit exercise into your schedule?

5. After a long day at work, the last thing my flesh wants to do is exercise. I am exhausted and tired. Can you relate? How can you prevent the easy chair from jeopardizing you getting the fresh air you need to clear your mind?

Chapter 4

Clear Your Conscience

"The goal of this command is love, which comes from a
pure heart and a good conscience and a sincere faith."

- I TIMOTHY 1:5

When someone says, "I sleep really well every night," another will often reply, "You must have a clear conscience." There is a lot of truth in that statement because a clean conscience brings peace of mind.

Acting against our conscience will cause tension in our inner lives. We can power through it, but the underlying stress of it will follow us wherever we go. We must come clean with God and get right with Him. Then we can be at peace again.

If we violate our consciences repeatedly, then we run the risk of developing a hard heart, or worse yet, a seared conscience. A hard heart is unable to experience the goodness of God. The seared conscience is unable to discern right from wrong. This inability to connect with Jesus will produce an anxious life.

God can break through all of those self-constructed walls and bring us peace. It's a painful process having to address our sins and come clean with God, but many can testify to the deep peace God brought them when they did.

If left unaddressed, a guilty conscience will agitate our spirit and add fuel to our inner chat room where self-talk keeps us stuck living in our thoughts. We were created to live from the heart with a calm mind and clarity of thought.

How Is the Conscience Cleared?

Believers can have their consciences cleansed through confession of their sins. The blood of Jesus Christ purifies us. In Hebrews 9:14 we read, "How much more, then, will the blood of Christ, who through the eternal Spirit offered himself unblemished to God, cleanse our consciences from acts that lead to death so that we may serve the living God!"

In the New Covenant, God has already forgiven us from all of our sins. We are completely forgiven in Jesus. God has declared us sinners righteous by His grace. We have been justified freely. This is our position in Christ.

But to experience what we already have in Christ, we need to practice confession of our sin. It sanctifies our soul and frees us from guilt and shame. The Holy Spirit removes the guilt, lifts the burden, banishes all condemnation, and sets us, the prisoner, free. This is a crucial step to having peace with God. It is foundational in discipleship.

We all sin every day. Jesus taught us how to have our consciences cleared daily and our heart renewed. In the model prayer, Jesus taught us to pray, "Forgive us our debts." Asking God sincerely to forgive us will clear our conscience.

This is called a prayer of confession. It unburdens and frees us. "If we claim to be without sin, we deceive ourselves and the truth is not in us. If we confess our sins, he is faithful and just, and will forgive us our sins and purify us from all unrighteousness" (I John 1:8–9).

Confession is a spiritual shower we need every day. It cleanses us. When I become aware of my sin during the day, I will whisper to God a confession of my lust, greed, upset, gossip, envy, prejudice, selfishness, impatience, deceit, or whatever else I may have thought, done, or neglected to do.

A sincere, humble "Lord, I am sorry, please forgive me," will cleanse the heart and reset our mind. The quicker we do this, the better we will be.

When I get to the confession part of my nightly prayers, I ask the Lord to examine me and show me any shortcomings I missed during the day so that I may confess them to Him, learn from them, and let them go.

Confession is not to "keep up" my salvation, but to keep me clean and current in my relationship with Jesus. We need daily renewal. This cleansing makes us holy. It's one of the reasons we pray.

It's All About Relationship

When a child knowingly disobeys a clear boundary set by the parent, then a face-to-face accounting must take place to move forward. Parents train children in what is good and right for them. They do not let willful violations of crucial directions slide—like not playing on the road, or not lying to your teacher.

Parents know that children must fess up, take responsibility for their choices, and change their minds. It's for their good. Parents love their children too much to leave them to their own devices.

The relationship between a loving parent and child is in discord until this matter is addressed and resolved. The parent isn't at rest until the child gets in sync with the parent's will for that child. It's the loving and right thing to do.

When it's resolved, good and close relations resume, and the child has learned valuable lessons in the process. This is part of a highly functioning household.

Our heavenly Father has a similar agenda in teaching us the good and right path. We often fail. He is patient—and persistent. He is gracious—and truthful. He is gentle—and firm. He knows what it takes to lead us in the way everlasting.

It's His responsibility to train us up in the way we should go. He is not angry. He simply loves us too much to leave us to our own devices.

So, if we knowingly and willfully disobeyed God, then we must return to our point of departure, confess our sin, and be cleansed from unrighteousness.

Repentance

Confession clears the conscience then repentance brings our mind into agreement with God. Repentance is as essential to Christian growth as any spiritual practice in the Bible. When it comes from the heart, nothing will restore peace to you like confession and repentance because it leads us back into harmony with God.

It's refreshing to the soul. "Repent, then, and turn to God, so that your sins may be wiped out, that times of refreshing may come from the Lord" (Acts 3:19-20).

This daily practice aligns our life to the Word of God and draws us close to God. As the Scripture reveals to us right from wrong, our mind is to come into agreement with the Word. Then, our attitude and actions will follow.

It's a practice that responds to the Word and the conviction of the Holy Spirit. It should be viewed as a normal, regular, and important part of growing in Christ. A.W. Pink wrote, "The Christian who has stopped repenting has stopped growing."[3]

The peace of Christ deepens in us over time as we respond to the Word of God with repentance. If we are not

3 A.W. Pink Quotes, Good Reads, www.goodreads.com.

responding to the Word by applying it to our heart, our heart will be dulled to the movement of the Spirit and tension will result. But if we seek to be in tune with God's Word and our hearts are pliable, then we will be transformed by the working of the Holy Spirit.

Kindness and Repentance

God's kind heart behind the call to repentance can be found in Paul's letter to the Romans where he wrote, "Or do you show contempt for the riches of his kindness, forbearance and patience, not realizing that God's kindness is intended to lead you to repentance?" (Romans 2:4).

When you hear the word "repent," don't think about the caricature of a sharp-tongued, fiery preacher condemning you from the Bible. Think of the kindness of Jesus patiently and intentionally calling you to adopt His better way. That trustworthy vision of Jesus and His Word will help you make the change and follow Him.

The Holy Spirit convinces us to change and take God's way. His goal is to move us onto the Father's agenda. We can resist him. That's freedom of the will.

But God's will is convincing and compelling, able to turn our hearts to the right. For this we should be thankful. He is not indifferent toward us but wants our best.

I was standing in a creek bed on a golf course when it hit me that cheating wasn't good. I was tempted to move my ball a few feet to a nice patch of grass to hit my next shot. I knew it wasn't right, but I didn't realize it wasn't good. I would often cheat on my score—anything to prove myself.

But something clicked in me that day. I was just fooling myself. My score wasn't true or real. My conscience said, "Play it where it lies." I did. I changed. I gained some integrity on the golf course. It felt much better, more peaceful.

I needed to apply it to school and everything else. That would come later. But in that moment, I took a big step as a young person toward the good and better way.

Having a vision of what you are repenting to is vital. We are repenting to a better way. Embrace the good God is calling you to. Then you will more readily let go of your old pattern. It's the Father's plan for an abundant life for His children, a more trustworthy path to follow.

Obedience may cost us. In our mind, we may have to sacrifice something. But trust Him. The pain of loving God and others will turn into joy just as sure as the resurrection turned a man of sorrows into a risen King. Your obedience will give you peace of mind and open doors to a better future.

Self-Knowledge Is Pivotal

We can't treat symptoms and expect to get better. Anxiety is a symptom of our anxious thoughts and beliefs that miss the mark. *Hamartia*, the Greek word for sin, literally means "to miss the mark." It comes from archery. When an archer shot an arrow at a target and missed it, it was called *hamartia* or sin.

We tend to focus on getting our actions right. That's crucial. But often our actions and our emotional state stem from our underlying thoughts and beliefs. That's where sin is conceived. That's the root of the problem.

And as any gardener knows, you've got to get the root out or that undesirable weed will reappear and cause trouble again. Get our heart beliefs right and our thoughts will come into alignment with God. Righteousness and peace follow.

God knows all our ways. It is a wonderful and sobering thought that God knows everything about us.

David wrote: "You have searched me, LORD, and you know me. You know when I sit and when I rise; you perceive my thoughts from afar. You discern my going out and my lying down; you are familiar with all my ways" (Psalm 139:1–4).

God knows us much better than we know ourselves. Part of the conviction the Holy Spirit gives us is God giving us knowledge of ourselves—knowledge of underlying thoughts and motives. Without this conviction, we would be hopelessly lost in self-deception.

Like David, we should desire this self-knowledge so we can break free and grow. That's why David finishes Psalm 139 with, "Search me, God, and know my heart; test me and know my anxious thoughts. See if there is any offensive way in me, and lead me in the way everlasting" (Psalm 139:23–24).

We have anxious, offensive thoughts that we don't want to admit, so we cover them up. Any persistent thought that misses the mark of God's Word will result in some level of anxiety. Unless we ask God to bring those anxious thoughts to the surface and into the light, we cannot change.

I may need to admit "I am afraid of someone" or "I envy that person" or "I feel like nobody cares about me." Or I may need to confess something childish that scares me. Shame keeps thoughts like that covered up. But, getting real gets results with God.

Practice openness and transparency with God. Our underlying motives and attitudes influence our emotional state and our actions. Only God knows our heart. Confession and repentance are all good from beginning to end. They result in good works and peaceful emotions.

If you are like me, you may have neglected this important practice for too long. My stuff built up over time. I needed to deal with some things from my past and get current with God.

My Big Breakthrough

Most of us either have had or need to have a "come to Jesus" moment, a time when we face the painful reality of our sinful past. When we have willfully chosen to do what we know is wrong, we need to address it to be at peace with God.

I wasn't even aware of all that I needed to bring before God in confession. Eventually, it caught up with me. I had a hard heart. Bible study just wasn't producing change in me or helping me as much it should have.

God let me know through a Scripture given to me by a minister friend that God would be at work to turn my "heart of stone into a heart of flesh" (Ezekiel 36:26). I was brought to tears many times during this incredible season of my life-changing transformation.

One of the biggest moments happened unexpectedly.

I faced the reality of my own death and judgment without having to go through a life-threatening experience like a car wreck or a cancer diagnosis. I read the near-death experience of Howard Storm in his book *My Descent into Death*. And my life flashed before me.

God used Storm's account to remove the layers of deceit in me and reveal my sin. God convicted me of my own judgment day from reading the account of Storm's life review that Jesus showed him.

Storm saw the vanity and selfishness of his life. He observed himself in scenes with his family and in career that revealed his inner thoughts and self-centered desires for acclaim.

While there was no condemnation, only love coming from Jesus, Storm was broken over viewing his life as it was laid bare before him. He wasn't enduring judgment for his sin, but he was getting a look at the futility of his life and the pain it caused others.[4]

The Holy Spirit used this account to break me. I knew I had been just as selfish and prideful as Howard Storm. I came to Jesus uncovered and naked. Out of a healthy fear of God, I took off the fig leaves that were hiding my shame. God graciously brought the reality of my own life review right before me.

As I looked at some of the events in my life, I could see my ulterior motives, secret thoughts, fantasies, lies, deceit, anger.... I saw selfishness and a lack of genuine love in decision-making. I was unmasked by the Holy Spirit. It was very painful to see.

I knew the day would come when I too would have to see that review with Jesus. Even though Howard Storm said he felt no condemnation and only love from Jesus, he had to face the reality of his own misguided thoughts, motives, and actions.

When I saw some of my life from childhood scenes to present day, I repented in many tears and much brokenness.

---

4 Howard Storm, *My Descent into Death,* (New York: Doubleday, 2005), 31.

With every scene the Lord brought to my mind, I felt tremendous sorrow.

In one scene, I cussed my loving mother; in another, I took out my anger on my brother. In yet another scene, I was manipulating the church. I also understood that the motivations underlying my life were not pure—not by a long shot.

The pain was acute, but at the same time, with each confession, I experienced a love so intense I could scarcely take it in—it was the mercy of God flooding my soul. It was a severe mercy, a grace that was greater than all my sin and shame.

Guilt was pouring out, and God's mercy was streaming in. When my tears came down, God's love flowed in. Cleansing happened, shame lifted, and I was free. It changed my life.

This appointed time cleared my mind, purified my heart, and allowed me to experience intimacy with God. I would not be the same again.

God says through the prophet Isaiah: "'I live in a high and holy place, but also with the one who is contrite and lowly in spirit, to revive the spirit of the lowly and to revive the heart of the contrite…I have seen their ways, but I will heal them; I will guide them and restore comfort to Israel's mourners, creating praise on their lips. Peace, peace, to those far and near,' says the LORD. 'And I will heal them'" (Isaiah 57:15, 18–19).

God lives with "the one who is contrite and lowly in spirit." He comforts mourners and brings praise to their lips. It's such a paradox—God has chosen to dwell in the hearts of lowly and broken sinners.

That's the conscience-clearing power of genuine confession. It brought me close to God, gave me a heart of flesh, and established a beachhead of peace in my soul.

David's Breakthrough

These God-ordained, house-cleaning moments are for those of us who have a hard heart or who have not kept our relationship with God current. Or maybe we glossed over a willful sin—knowing full well it was wrong but did it anyway. We must return to the point of our departure from God's way, confess it to Him, experience forgiveness, and get back on track.

King David had such a moment. He committed adultery with Bathsheba and had her husband killed in battle. He then moved on by taking Bathsheba to be his wife.

Nine months later, God sent Nathan the prophet to David, and the prophet used a parable to confront the king: a rich man who had many flocks of sheep took a poor man's only sheep and killed it to eat.

David, a former shepherd, was so angered by this story that he responded, "As surely as the LORD lives, the man who did this must die! He must pay for that lamb four times over because he did such a thing and had no pity" (II Samuel 12:5–6).

Nathan then literally pointed to David and uttered the chilling words, "You are the man!" This Word of God cut David through like a knife and cut through the fog of his self-deception. This act of God laid bare David's sin before him to awaken him to come clean with God.

David responded by writing, "Have mercy on me, O God, according to your unfailing love; according to your great compassion blot out my transgressions. Wash away all my iniquity and cleanse me from my sin. For I know my transgressions, and my sin is always before me" (Psalm 51:1–3).

David had an awakening. He saw his sin as God saw it and repented. When we view our sin the way God views our sin, we will shudder and repent. The repulsing nature of our sin becomes clear when our eyes are opened.

We will then turn to Jesus and cry out for mercy. He forgives and cleanses us. God's kindness draws us to an infinitely better way to live. We receive a vision of righteousness and peace, and we run to it. We are left with an awe and reverence for God.

We must believe in the gracious nature of God. David came to the One whom he had offended because he believed in the God of mercy. He came in holy fear to the throne of grace and asked for forgiveness. It's always granted to those who come to Him with a contrite heart. It's God's desire to accomplish that in us. He loves us.

We Can't Let Go of the Past Until...

How many of us have tried to let go of the past but it still affects us? We have to *resolve* the past to be free from it.

We cannot just say "I let it go" because it's bonded to us until we deal with it. The past, if left unredeemed, will affect us every day of our lives even if we just forget about it and move on—like David did.

In Christ, we can be unbound, set free, and liberated from our past guilt through confession and repentance. Then, we *can* let it go, move forward, and it will not affect us anymore. Through Jesus, we can live with a clean conscience.

A Moral Inventory

If you are not current with God, clearing your conscience can be accomplished by doing a moral inventory. Twelve-step ministries call it a "fearless moral inventory" because it takes gut-wrenching honesty to face and confess the shameful things we have done or harbored in our hearts.

It's a crucial step in being free. Sin, guilt, and hurt remain in us until we confess and bring them out into the flow of God's cleansing tide.

In a moral inventory, we write down all the wrong we have done and the secrets we've lived with but hidden. This soul-searching practice has to also uncover the false pretenses and selfish motives underlying our hurtful attitudes, actions, and addictions. This is to be our confession before God. It takes humble transparency and Holy Spirit guidance.

C.S. Lewis wrote in *The Problem of Pain*, "We have a strange illusion that mere time cancels sin. But mere time does nothing either to the fact or to the guilt of a sin."[5]

Often, in a retreat or youth camp setting, the participants are led in a form of this moral inventory and confession. At an appropriate time, in a Holy-Spirit inspired moment, they are asked to search their hearts and write out their secret sins on a piece of paper. They take time to uncover what they've done and confess it to the Lord.

Then they are directed to let it go to Jesus—maybe by throwing it in a trash can, putting it in a fire, or nailing it to a cross. The purpose of this is to facilitate a spiritual transaction in the heart, cleansing them from guilt and thus reviving the soul.

This inner transaction unbinds the soul from sin and clears the conscience. It results in a restored relationship with God, a renewed spirit, purer thoughts, and a restful soul. God has already forgiven us, but we need to *experience* this forgiveness to have our consciences cleansed.

Often, we have to work with a mentor, pastor, or small group for that purpose—to cut to the chase, quit lying to ourselves, and uproot evil, pain, lies, deceitful desires, and impure motives.

[5] Goodreads quote, www.goodreads.com

This takes a willingness to be exposed and an openness to brokenness. We have to get really desperate to get really honest. Then, this moral inventory can work to awaken and revive us.

Jesus knew that many people would avoid this, evidenced when He taught, "This is the verdict: Light has come into the world, but people loved darkness instead of light because their deeds were evil. Everyone who does evil hates the light, and will not come into the light for fear that their deeds will be exposed" (John 3:19–20).

We can't expect to just move on with God in a close relationship with Him without honesty and confession. The self-justifying wall of deceit within us can be very thick. We have willed it into existence to hide our anxiety-producing sin and shame.

But, letting down that wall with Jesus will bring our sin to light, allowing God's grace to come in and vanquish its hold on us. In the next verse, Jesus taught, "Whoever lives by the truth comes into the light, so that it may be seen plainly that what they have done has been done in the sight of God" (John 3:21).

Someone said that sobriety is 10% about the alcohol and 90% about honesty. I would say something similar, that our salvation and sanctification are 90% about honesty and 10% about knowledge.

Knowledge is easily available, but true honesty is hard to come by. We need God's help. We cannot even be honest with ourselves on our own, but with the Holy Spirit we can.

Sin cannot live in the presence of God. In the light of Truth, sin is exposed for what it is, then it loses its sway over us in the sight of God.

Willingly bring what is hidden in shame into the Light to be cleansed by the love and holiness of God. In His presence, there is fullness of joy and the absence of sin. The power of the blood of Jesus will heal us.

Questions for Reflection and Application

1. I John 1:9 says, "If we confess our sins, he is faithful and just and will forgive us our sins and purify us from all unrighteousness." How often do you confess specific sins to God and ask for forgiveness?

    a. Read Psalm 51. Write down the benefits David describes in his prayer of repentance.

    b. Recall an experience you have had with confessing your sin. Write down the effects it had on your life.

2. Confession brings sin into the open with God and repentance turns our life to the right path of God. What could you do to more fully align your life to the Word and will of God? Is there something the Holy Spirit is convicting you of that you need to get right in your life? What steps can you take to accomplish this?

3. What is a moral inventory?

    a. Do you feel like you are current in your relationship with God? Or do you feel like you need to come clean with God over some things you have done in your past that were wrong?

    b. On paper, write out what comes to mind as you reflect upon your past sins and failures. Take time with this exercise. In honesty and without fear, let your secrets and motives as well as the actions and attitudes be expressed.

c. Do you still feel guilty for things you have done in your past? Are you ready to confess those to God and experience His forgiveness and cleansing? If so, get on your knees before God if you are able. Ask Him to forgive you. Then let it go to Jesus who paid the price for your sins. (Then you can throw away your paper too.) Describe your prayer experience below.

Chapter 5

Renew Your Mind

*"I remain confident of this: I will see the goodness of
the LORD in the land of the living."*

- PSALM 27:13

It's been said that the mind is the devil's playground. But
our minds are God's holy ground where His Spirit is to
rule and where lies are to be defeated. Our minds can be the
place where we take every thought captive and submit them
to Jesus. This chapter will teach you how to do that.

You can't fight this battle and win with willpower and effort. The battle is won by the Lord. He demolishes
strongholds with the power of His truth.

The world realizes the struggle is in the mind. They
know thoughts get out of control and cause anxiety. Many
resources are available for self-help and mind control, but
our flesh is beyond help. It's always self-centered and self-
absorbed. It knows nothing else.

But we have the mind of Christ, the Holy Spirit of truth
who can govern our thoughts and instill peace of mind. We
are to act in concert with Him to assimilate God's Word into

our view of reality. This work of God in governing our minds will bring us peace.

Paul wrote, "The mind governed by the flesh is death, but the mind governed by the Spirit is life and peace" (Romans 8:6).

Since peace results when our minds are ruled by the Holy Spirit, we need to give Him control, ask Him to teach us the Word. We need to listen to His voice.

We are to view prayer and Bible study as the school of the Spirit. He is our teacher, our Wonderful Counselor. We are to be in His classroom. There are powerful spiritual truths to be spiritually discerned. The Spirit can enlighten us to really know the truth.

In your quiet time, before reading the Word, give Jesus your mind. Yield your thoughts to Him. Ask Him to teach you. He will give you insight and spiritual understanding.

When we do this, our outlook will become hopeful and our attitude peaceful. We will realize that there is purpose in suffering, redemption in failure, and light in the darkness.

"We are hard pressed on all sides, but not crushed; perplexed but not in despair; persecuted but not forsaken; struck down but not destroyed" (II Corinthians 4:8–9). During life's most difficult challenges, these are the thoughts that transform our emotions and fill us with peace.

A Nutritional Diet

Everyone knows that what we take into our bodies will affect our health and well-being in the future. The same is true for our mental and emotional health. Each day, we are to take in what is pure and produces good thoughts. "Set your mind on what the Spirit desires" (Romans 8:5).

Anxiety will reign if we don't set some limits around what we put into our minds. For the most part, what we take in is under our control. We will be molded by our thoughts.

Paul writes of the incredible impact of good thoughts on our peace: "Finally, brothers and sisters, whatever is true, whatever is noble, whatever is right, whatever is pure, whatever is lovely, whatever is admirable—if anything is excellent or praiseworthy—think about such things. Whatever you have learned or received or heard from me, or seen in me—put it into practice. And the God of peace will be with you" (Philippians 4:8–9).

The above verse teaches that the God of peace will be with those who think about pure and praiseworthy things. Let's count our blessings more often than we recall our critics, ponder the Word more than we listen to the world, and dial in to powerful preaching more than we tune in to political pundits. We can change our thinking by changing the input.

What goes into your mind determines the state of your mind and emotions. Give God your ear. Listen to Him and put a limit on your intake of worldly chatter.

The world is full of discord because of mankind's estrangement from God. We can let that discordant worldview play in our mind or we can consider the abundant blessings, the lofty purposes, and the unshakeable hope we have in Christ.

We can keep our entertainment noble, our music pure, our books admirable, and our conversations lovely. Which of these inputs can you adjust to become more praiseworthy?

Make that your practice starting today. What can you let go of or add to make your mental diet more spiritually nourishing? These inputs can speak into your life and lighten your outlook with hope and peace.

Season Your Speech With Grace

I used to initiate or join in negative conversations. I would criticize a coach, condemn a fallen sinner, complain about a leader, gossip about a neighbor, excoriate a politician, judge a fellow believer...Even conversations that began well would often turn negative about the world.

It even seemed like a "Christian way to talk." But the enemy deceived me. I didn't realize how much this bad practice poisoned my mind and my environment.

Then I started to notice that peaceful people didn't talk this way. They also had wisdom, character, and the respect of people. I became consciously aware of how my critical conversations corrupted me.

I remember making a commitment to keep my conversation free of gossip, complaining, criticizing, or judging anyone. It became a spiritual practice.

This change made a huge impact in the level of peace and kindness in my soul. It's now my lifestyle. I haven't been perfect, but I definitely have more peace from this practice. I intentionally disciplined my conversations with the goal of letting "my speech always be gracious" (Colossians 4:6).

The practice of bridling the tongue will keep the stress out of our spirit and take the drama out of our lives.

Mental Strongholds

Even with our best intentions to think more noble thoughts, there can be deep-rooted lies, dyed-in-the-wool beliefs, and anxious underlying thoughts that all the discipline in the world can't shake. These mental strongholds corrupt our best efforts at prayer, thinking noble thoughts, and having peace of mind. It's a daily source of inner discord and stress.

This means that there is an unredeemed area of our mind that needs to be uncovered, identified, and submitted to Jesus.

Paul writes about this: "The weapons we fight with are not the weapons of the world. On the contrary, they have divine power to demolish strongholds. We demolish arguments and every pretension that sets itself up against the knowledge of God, and we take captive every thought to make it obedient to Christ" (II Corinthians 10:4–5).

The divine power to demolish strongholds—pretensions and lies—is taking captive those deeply rooted, recurrent thoughts and submitting them to Jesus.

Then, we can do what the Father instructed His followers to do at the Mount of Transfiguration: "While he was still speaking, a bright cloud covered them, and a voice from the cloud said, 'This is my Son, whom I love; with him I am well pleased. Listen to him!'" (Matthew 17:5).

When the Father puts an exclamation mark on the end of a command, it's super important. When we submit to Jesus the lies that cause our inner discord, we are to listen for His reply. He will impart truth that will demolish the stronghold that the lie has on our mind. Peace will follow.

Our Past Influences Our View of Reality

Specific fears come from lie-based beliefs. Those beliefs often form early in life and become our mindset, which filters our view of reality. Some beliefs were hardwired into us in our formative period.

Some of these fearful thoughts developed in childhood disappear as we age. We may have just grown out of some phobias, like fear of the dark.

Yet some things remain with us, imprinted in our souls. These strongholds can't just be grown out of, let go, or shaken off. We continue to be triggered by certain situations and become anxious. We must identify their root, submit the lies to Jesus, and be renewed by His Spirit.

My dad was hospitalized with Battle Fatigue, now called PTSD, during and shortly after World War II. He endured jungle warfare in the battles to retake the Philippines. The combat was close and fierce. At night, the Japanese would slip out of their positions in the cover of dark and use knives in silent attacks on the soldiers.

I learned from my uncle that one of my dad's friends died right beside him in one such attack. Dad had a God-given reason to fear in those moments. That fear gave him powerful rushes of adrenaline to fight the battle.

But when the fight is over, the mental battle sometimes continues even though the threat is no longer present. Anxiety can be triggered by situations that our subconscious mind associates as similar to a traumatic life experience. It's a protection mechanism.

For some people who have endured trauma of one kind or another, this protection mechanism never turns off. The filter is there just under the surface and tests everything that is happening in their lives to determine whether it's a threat.

Position Yourself to Hear from God

My dad's example illustrates how we need to bring our difficult experiences to Jesus who can renew our minds and relieve us from having to be "on guard" all the time. Whether it was childhood trauma or a horrific experience in adulthood, the Holy Spirit can help restore our minds and bring them into the light of truth.

It's a process. It takes great care and patience, but with Jesus in the process, a renewal of our minds absolutely can happen.

Normal past fearful experiences can also trigger anxiety in us through this same type of mental association. So, to be free from a specific anxiety, we must first identify and address the root cause, the associated life event.

In those fearful experiences, identify the anxious thoughts that were impressed upon you. Then submit them to Jesus and listen to Him. Often, His truth will come to our understanding to renew our mind.

Put Off the Old and Put on the New

Take comfort in the knowledge that God desires us to overcome and will accomplish that work in us if we cooperate with Him. We must intentionally put ourselves in a position to receive help from His Spirit. God sent His Spirit for this very purpose—to sanctify us in truth.

Jesus prayed to the Father for us: "But when he, the Spirit of truth, comes, he will guide you into all the truth. He will not speak on his own; he will speak only what he hears, and he will tell you what is yet to come" (John 16:13).

God is at work to sanctify our minds in truth. Being free of worry and anxiety happens the same way that we grow in Christ—put off the old and put on the new. As born-again followers of Christ, we are new creations.

Paul writes, "You were taught, with regard to your former way of life, to put off your old self, which is being corrupted by its deceitful desires; to be made new in the attitude of your minds; and to put on the new self, created to be like God in true righteousness and holiness" (Ephesians 4:22–24).

We are to put off our old beliefs, which are corrupted by deceitful thinking, and put on new beliefs in alignment with the truth. This is how we overcome. This is how we grow. Purity forms, love expands, peace deepens, and joy permeates as we are transformed by the renewing of our minds.

While I learned these biblical principles early in my pastoral ministry, I did not understand how to apply them to bring freedom from my recurrent specific anxieties and strongholds. Nothing seemed to help.

I could not shake these particular sins and fears even though I read the Bible, prayed, and had fellowship with other Christians. I was stuck. I didn't know how to "put off" the deceit and "put on" the new self.

A recurrent anger issue led me to a ministry that is now called Transformation Prayer Ministry (transformationprayer.org). In training sessions, they taught me biblical principles I already believed, but I didn't know how to apply those truths most effectively to my struggle with negative emotions.

I will share testimonies of how my wife and I found freedom from specific anxieties through the applications I learned from Transformation Prayer Ministry. Online they have quality training videos and helpful resources. It's all free. I don't represent them, and my comments are based my own understanding. I am simply one of many who have benefited from their ministry. Bottom line, it's all about Jesus and making us more like Him.

From Flying with Fear to Flying Free

"Then you will know the truth, and the truth will set you free" (John 8:32).

Flying always scared me. I was okay with it as long as the plane felt steady, but any bumps or sudden moves caused me to feel like things were out of control, and we were going to crash.

Little bumps happen on most every flight, and they alarmed me. With turbulence, I was a nervous wreck. Whenever the plane undulated a bit, I would try to sit real still so as not to cause any further swaying of the plane.

Hilarious—right? Well, I felt like we would crash and die when the plane jostled so I was doing my part to keep it from swaying. That was my trigger point—when I felt like the plane was out of control.

I would look around at fellow passengers who did not seem one bit concerned and think, "Don't you care? Don't you realize we very well may crash?"

I would see them reading, gaming on an iPad, or just napping while the plane jostled around. They seemed unaware of the pending crash that could happen any moment.

Kids didn't even seem concerned. *What is wrong with those people?* I would say to myself. After the flight was over, I would think, *What's wrong with me?*

Anxiety is intense worry and fear about everyday situations. Sometimes we see things logically and can step away from the situation and see no reason to fear. But when we think about entering the situation, we feel the fear. It's totally real to us.

We get uptight and panicked over something many people do routinely. We know this, but we see no way to control this illogical feeling. It can be frustrating because we know better—intellectually, that is. Other people have no problem with it, so we're back to wondering, *What's wrong with me?*

I remember reminding myself of how much safer flying is than any other mode of transportation, especially driving. I read the statistics and told myself, *These pilots fly most days of the year and oftentimes the same routes. This airline flies my route every day and nothing bad happens. What do you have to fear?*

This rational knowledge did nothing to alleviate my anxiety. For some reason, I didn't trust the knowledge. I thought I did, but once the plane encountered turbulence, I panicked; my heart raced uncontrollably. Still, I sucked it up and flew anyway. I flew in fear, but I flew. Some people call that courage. I don't. I had anxiety.

We had a long way to travel from Kentucky to Minnesota to visit Dana's parents, but her dad worked for an airline, and we got complementary tickets. I couldn't pass that up. It was too hard for me to admit to anyone that I feared flying.

On one flight, I decided to apply what I had learned from Transformation Prayer Ministry to my anxiety. I thought my mind might be associating a past fearful moment with the present. The negative emotion was not my problem. It was a symptom or the fruit of a false belief that was rooted in an experience. My past influenced my perception of the present.

On one particular flight to visit Dana's parents, we encountered turbulence, and I felt anxiety and panic. I focused on the anxiety then simply allowed the memory I was associating this event with to come to the surface.

I didn't go looking for it. I just asked myself, "What does this panicked feeling remind me of?" My mind subconsciously associated it anyway, so it didn't take long for the memory to come to me.

The memory was of my childhood friend Joe getting a brand-new Honda XR-75 motorcycle. As I slowly began to recall the details, I remembered he asked me if I wanted to go for a ride. I agreed, hopped on the back, and we took off riding on a gravel road by his house. Joe started flying down that road, and I felt the motorcycle sliding as we went around the curves.

I was afraid and thought, "Joe doesn't know what he is doing! He's out of control. We are going to wreck, and I am going to die." I told him, "Hey, Joe slow down. We're going to wreck." But he just laughed and spun ahead.

I was certain that I was going to die on that curvy gravel road that day. It made an impression on me: *Don't trust anyone driving again.* I was so relieved to be finished with that joy ride. I didn't want to go on a ride like that ever again.

But actually, I did go on a ride like that again many times—except there was one difference—I was driving the motorcycle! No fear then. I could careen around corners like Joe, fly down the same road, do jumps, climb hills, slide a little, but all without fear…Why?

I trusted my own driving, and I had no reason to think I was going to die. I knew what I was doing. I was in control. I felt fear only when someone else was driving, and I was the passenger. Then, it didn't take much for me to be triggered and feel tremendous, gripping fear.

Well, you can see how my mind associated that experience I had as a kid with anything remotely similar. The lie-based belief I held was, "We will wreck and die because we are out of control. The driver cannot be trusted."

Any similar experience for me would be seen through that lens and interpreted as a scary situation. Based on an experience, I accepted the lie that you can't trust anyone but yourself behind the wheel. Identifying what I believed (the lie) and why I believed it (the memory) put me in a position to submit the belief to Jesus and listen to Him.

This false belief I had was the real reason I did all of the driving in our marriage. When my wife Dana drove, any slight drift or unexpected move would cause panic in me. When any little thing would happen, I would feel out of control like we were going to wreck and die.

If I was at the wheel, those things didn't bother me. I could trust myself, but no one else. One of the reasons we feel like we have to be in control is that to be otherwise is to live in fear.

No amount of empirical evidence could change the way I felt. No reliable facts (like women having fewer accidents) could dispel my fear. Any unexpected movement in a car triggered my anxiety if someone else was driving. My mind subconsciously associated it with my "near-death experience" on the back of Joe's motorcycle.

So, on that plane, as I was remembering the ride with Joe and feeling the fear, I asked myself, *What do you feel is true?* I answered myself, *We are out of control. We are going to wreck, and I am going to die.*

Then I asked, *What else do you feel?* I examined my motive and answered, *I don't trust the driver.* There was the root lie and why I believed it. This anxious thought formed the way I perceived riding with Joe and, after that, with anybody else.

I stayed in that memory moment and said, "Lord, I feel like we are going to wreck and die because Joe's driving is out of control. I don't trust him. Would you show me the truth?" Then the Lord said, "Trust him."

I didn't hear audible words, but that truth came to my understanding in that memory. Jesus gave me that revelation. Trust for God in the situation and for Joe came into my experience. Jesus brought the truth I needed to fully know.

I let that sink in. I trusted God. I trusted Joe. I was confident and at peace with him driving. This simple, biblical truth took hold and produced peace and calm in me.

Did this change how I felt on that plane ride I was in the middle of? I felt like it did, but I wasn't completely sure, because we were almost at our destination and the plane ride had become smooth.

On our return flight, however, we encountered turbulence, and I distinctly remember thinking to myself, *Hey this isn't bad. Actually, this is pretty cool. It's been a boring flight; now, it is getting a little exciting!*

I was shocked. I couldn't believe I was feeling that way. There was no anxiety, but instead a little excitement. Why? I trusted God and the pilot. I knew it. The truth I had received from Jesus now informed my perception. My mind had been renewed. I was flying free for the first time!

This truth, this view of reality has held true over the past twenty years. I have been anxious about other things in life but not flying. Why? My mind has been changed in the place where I needed clarity. I can discern God's will and His ways in this situation.

"Do not conform to the pattern of this world, but be transformed by the renewing of your mind. Then you will be able to test and approve what God's will is—his good, pleasing, and perfect will" (Romans 12:2).

The Holy Spirit governs my view of this segment of my world so that it is in agreement with His "good, pleasing, and perfect will." God freed me from an ingrained false belief and the corresponding irrational fear that emanated from it.

No maintenance was needed to keep me at peace in that situation. I don't have to "get prayed up" to fly. My mind has been washed in the Living Word of truth. I have no more anxious thoughts about flying. The Word of the Lord endures forever.

When circumstances are viewed through the lens of God's Word, nothing threatens us. "Knowing" the truth is made possible by the help of the Spirit of Christ. To know the truth is to experience the truth.

The truth can't be effective if it just remains something read on a page in our Bible. We do not come up with the truth on our own. And we can't plant the truth into our minds either. We know truth because God makes it known by His Spirit through His Word. That's why Bible study and prayer go together.

God does not withhold the truth from us. We must simply ask. But we need to be specific when we ask God to remove our anxious thoughts.

The best way I have found to do that is to first identify the underlying belief that is causing my anxiety and why I believe it. Then I submit that root lie up to Jesus in prayer and have found that He will gladly demolish it with the truth. He withholds no good thing from His children.

I received unexpected benefits from that prayer in the airplane. After that, Dana could take turns driving with me on long trips. I started napping while she drove because I trusted God and her. I became at ease with her at the wheel.

Another surprising benefit became evident when, as a chaperone, I visited the Holiday World Theme Park in Indiana. I used to ride roller coasters with the youth of our church even though the rides scared me.

I did it because it was a great bonding experience with the young people. I did not want to miss out on that opportunity. I never let on that these rides scared me to death, but I never rode up front. That would have been too much to bear.

However, on this particular day at Holiday World, I spontaneously got in the line forming for the lead car on the roller coaster. I couldn't believe I was doing it.

I got in the front seat, settled in, and felt no fear. As the cars accelerated down the track and swung around the bend, my adrenalin rushed, my hands went up, my voice whooped, and I screamed with thrill and excitement. I was enjoying myself. I thought, *Wow, what a difference having no fear makes! Praise the Lord!*

What was the difference? I trusted God, the ride, and the people in charge; therefore, I did not feel like I was going to die. It wasn't a reckless disregard for danger, but a trust in God's will and a trustworthy operation.

Just a few months ago, I rode a corkscrew roller coaster and every other thrilling ride in a theme park with my teenage nieces. It was a fun and wholesome shared experience. We liked it so much that we decided to make it an annual custom.

Dana and Doctors

Dana had to see doctors often as a child for recurrent tonsillitis. She had good experiences with them and considered them to be pleasant and helpful. So, when her parents told her that she would be going to the hospital to have her tonsils removed, she didn't mind.

Medical professionals had all been very nice in Dana's visits to doctors' offices. Her mom was a nurse at another hospital. She associated people working in the medical field with goodness and help.

Dana was carefree and happy when admitted to the hospital the night before surgery. She even got to eat supper in the hospital with her mom and dad. She felt special. She had no worries about anything.

When they wheeled her into the operating room the next day, she was surrounded by a lot of people who were ready to serve and help her. Even though her parents were not there, she trusted the workers.

Then, without warning, someone placed a black mask on her face. It shocked and scared her. She recalls panicking and thinking, "I can't breathe. I'm struggling. They are pushing a mask on me!" She resisted, but they pushed it even tighter.

Dana thought, "They are killing me! And they don't care!" Dana felt like she had been tricked and ambushed. Then she lost consciousness.

What did Dana take in and perceive as true that day? Medical professionals have power over you. They cannot be trusted. You never know what they will do. They could kill you.

Is that the truth? No, but Dana felt like it was true. They didn't explain what was about to happen, so that is how she perceived reality that day as a young girl. She experienced those lies as real and true.

When that happens, the lies become a hard-wired belief in many people. That's why we can go all of our lives with a specific anxiety that has no logical reason. It doesn't really matter whether it makes sense or not. It feels true to us. Our mind perceives reality through that lens.

Some things learned by experience are hard to unlearn. Once the concrete sets up, it's hard to crack. These upsetting life experiences can leave their imprint on our mind and disorder our view of life situations. But Jesus can shine the Light of truth in our darkness, renew our minds, and dispel the fear.

After Dana's experience having her tonsils removed, she loathed having to see the doctors. She was suspicious of them. She made her mother promise before going to see any doctor that they would not give her a shot.

She was always uncomfortable in their office. Why? They have power over you. They will surprise you. They could kill you. That was her belief. That experience in the operating room had changed her.

Dana grew up and learned that medical professionals were good, but that logical information didn't affect how she felt. When we believe something to be true through experience, logical thinking cannot dislodge it from us even though we want it to. Our mind associates with what we experienced and that mental association is hard to break.

But "Jesus replied, 'What is impossible with man is possible with God'" (Luke 18:27).

After we married, I soon realized that Dana got very nervous visiting the doctor or dentist. After I learned about Transformation Prayer, I saw it as an opportunity to help her with her anxiety. She agreed.

I asked her if she knew what was causing her fear and nervousness when visiting medical professionals. She said she had no idea. I asked her to focus on her fear. She did, and then she prayed that God would search her and help her know the origin of these anxious thoughts. It wasn't long before she remembered her traumatic experience as a child in the operating room.

She recounted it out loud in prayer. I asked her what she felt like was true when she focused on the feelings in the memory. Her eventual response was, "They have power over me. They surprised me. They are killing me."

That's the belief she adopted from that experience. The doctors and nurses didn't teach her that. They didn't intend for her to believe that. It was her experience, her perception, and it continued to inform her in similar circumstances.

I asked Dana if she was willing to submit those beliefs to Jesus. She replied that she was willing. She told Jesus something like, "Jesus, even though I know now what they were doing, I still feel like it is true that they have power over me and can kill me. Would you show me the truth?"

Jesus replied with truth to her understanding, "They are not in control over you. No one is going to pull the plug on your life without My permission." Jesus renewed her mind by the washing of His Word.

For Dana, this emotional healing was more of a process. She had to walk it out and keep praying. When she was faced with a procedure or surgery that made her nervous, we would pray again about it. Dana would ask her doctor questions about things she was unsure of or confess to her doctor what she was anxious about.

Through prayer, the good medical experiences she began to have, and the compassionate care she often received, Dana came to see medical professionals as a blessing, as people who there are to help and serve her. And Dana came to truly know that her life is ultimately in God's hands.

It all starts with getting the help you need, praying through hurtful life experiences, and listening to Jesus who renews our minds.

Summary for Particular Anxieties

Difficult experiences can influence our perception of current life events. Anxious thoughts and beliefs stemming from these must be taken captive and submitted to the Lord. Jesus demolishes strongholds with the truth. This makes all the difference in renewing our mind through the washing of His Word.

To recap, when I feel really anxious about a specific situation, I…

1. Focus on the fear.
2. Ask myself what memory comes to mind as I feel the fear?
3. Feel the fear in the memory and ask, "What do I feel is true and why?"
4. Offer that up to Jesus and invite Him to reveal truth.

Sometimes, it is a process involving trial and error. But, if I am patient and continue to reflect and pray in this way, truth comes to me that changes the way I view threatening situations.

The simple, biblical, and profoundly peaceful truths like "God loves you" and "God is beside you" will take away our fears when planted by the Holy Spirit in the places where fear resides.

Questions for Reflection and Application

1. "The mind governed by the flesh is death, but the mind governed by the Spirit is life and peace" (Romans 8:6). What does this verse mean to you?

    a. Think about what you take into your mind each day. What are the inputs that result in worrisome thoughts?

    b. What are the inputs that result in peaceful thoughts?

    c. What adjustments to your viewing and listening habits would decrease your level of stress?

    d. What habit would help you have more peace?

2. "Let your conversation be always full of grace..." (Colossians 4:6).

    a. How do your conversations with people influence your stress level?

    b. Is there someone you talk to regularly where the conversation usually turns negative? How could you make those conversations more gracious?

    c. What is a commitment you could make to keep your talk more gracious?

3. Do you have a specific anxiety, like the fear of flying, that
    you feel the need to discover the root cause of? If so, de-
    scribe that specific anxiety and what triggers it.

    a. Think about that anxiety. How does it make you
        feel?
    b. Focus on that feeling for a moment. What
        memory comes to your mind?
    c. What happened and how did it make you feel?
        Write all your feelings.
    d. What do you feel is true in that memory and
        why? For instance, if you feel afraid, ask yourself
        why you feel afraid?
    e. Offer that statement up to Jesus and ask Him to
        show you the truth. Write down whatever comes
        to you.
    f. Do that with other memories that come to mind
        when you focus on the fear. Do this until peace
        comes to your heart. This may take several ses-
        sions of reflection and prayer.

Chapter 6

Refine Your Faith

"For everyone born of God overcomes the world. This is the victory that has overcome the world, even our faith."

I JOHN 5:4

The importance of faith in overcoming anxieties cannot be overstated. The above verse holds the key to overcoming the world—and that key is our faith. We are all called to victory through trusting in the One who overcame everything the world could throw at Him—injustice, death, false accusations, betrayal. Jesus imparts His victory to us through faith.

Peter walked on water but, after he began to sink, we read, "Immediately Jesus reached out his hand and caught him. 'You of little faith,' he said, 'why did you doubt?'" (Matthew 14:31).

Even Peter got no sympathy from Jesus for a lack of faith. But He will help us come to faith because God has chosen to work through faith to accomplish His purposes. A lack of trust in God and His Word causes the disharmony of our

d and our emotional state. Faith in the truth brings us in
une with our God of peace.

When We Doubt

Believers have saving faith, but our faith is not yet perfect,
fully formed, or completely pure. We still stress out, sin, and
have trouble believing God about our future and our family.
Our faith needs to be refined to enable us to grow and have
peace.

Boldness should mark our way because we believe "no
weapon formed against you shall prosper" (Isaiah 54:17). But
we have to grow into that, and this chapter will help you.

Many of us are facing challenges right now that cause
worry and anxiety. We believe God but feel like we are failing
in the faith department. We can become desperate or discouraged.

Some may be questioning themselves, wondering, *Why
can't I just trust God with this?* Others are asking themselves,
What's wrong with me?

Nothing is wrong with anyone who struggles with doubt.
These are normal growing pains experienced by every believer—from the first disciple to today. From the very first
moment we became a Christ-follower, we begin to learn what
it takes to live by faith. God is our teacher.

There will always be a crisis to take us from our faith to a
more fully formed faith. Paul wrote, "For in it the righteous-

ness of God is revealed from faith to faith; as it is written: 'But the righteous one will live by faith'" (Romans 1:17, NASB).

In His plan, we will all be stretched by tests and trials to make our faith more complete. For each individual, those tests will take different forms. One can believe God for one thing but not another. That's okay for the moment. It's where we are. But God is teaching us to trust Him in those pressing situations.

What Are We to Do in the Pressure?

We need to cry out like the man whose son was possessed by a demon, "Lord, I do believe: help me overcome my unbelief" (Mark 9:24). The father needed belief in Jesus that wasn't mingled with his unbelief to meet the demonic threat to his son.

The son he loved was being oppressed. He was desperate and felt helpless. Are you facing something beyond your ability to fix? Is it nothing like you have ever faced before? Do you have faith but doubts, too?

"Jesus asked the boy's father, 'How long has he been like this?' 'From childhood,' he answered. 'It has often thrown him into fire or water to kill him. But if you can do anything, take pity on us and help us.' 'If you can?' said Jesus. 'Everything is possible for one who believes.' Immediately the boy's father exclaimed, 'I do believe; help me overcome my unbelief!'" (Mark 9:21–24).

I can relate to this father. I do believe in Jesus, but there have been many challenges that I have faced when my old self-trusting nature came to the fore instead of my faith in Jesus. And with that came stress and anxiety. I wondered if it was going to be okay or if I was going to make it.

My faith needed to be purified. Trusting in my way would not be enough to overcome such a challenge. I wanted to believe in Jesus. I wanted to walk in the faith taught in Scripture.

In our challenges, God will call forth our faith in Jesus as we learn to let go of another layer of self-trust.

Our faith is refined during the trials and tests of our life. Tests clarify what we believe. It's a gut check. How are we going to respond to a challenging situation? God speaks through these tests.

David Jeremiah taught this: "It has been said that difficulties don't determine who we are. Rather, they reveal who we are."[6]

When God called me to leave my job, sell my condo, and serve in missions in Africa for two years, my faith was tested. I placed my faith in Jesus and His Word at salvation, but my faith hadn't yet fully formed to actually leave all that was familiar and go on this mission.

---

[6] Every Day with Jesus, CBN 2021, 266.

For two months, I kept my call a secret. All I could think about was that it would be a step into the unknown. That scared me.

I asked God for confirmation. He was silent. I realized He couldn't make my call any clearer. I needed to rise up, step out, and go.

God showed me one thing that I needed—that He would be with me. That made all the difference. I turned my face toward His call and never looked back. God gave me faith through His Word that opened my heart to the future. I obeyed by faith.

We sometimes see things from a purely natural or physical viewpoint. Worries arise because we lean on our sight. God is actively teaching us to live by trusting in Him. Tests expose our unbelief so that our faith can be refined.

How Our Faith Is Refined

When impure nuggets of gold were refined in New Testament times, they were placed inside a crucible over fire where the heat caused the common alloys to unbind or separate from the gold. The gold, which was heavier, sank to the bottom, and the slag rose to the top. The refiner then scraped off the slag and captured the gold in the bottom.

Peter wrote, "In this you rejoice, though now for a little while, if necessary, you have been grieved by various trials, so that the tested genuineness of your faith—more precious than gold that perishes though it is tested by fire—may be found to result in praise and glory and honor at the revelation of Jesus Christ" (I Peter 1:6–7, ESV).

Faith, which is more precious than gold, is refined through trials much the same way. The fire has to come to expose our false beliefs. We can't avoid this testing. We have to face it, give it an honest look, identify the false beliefs, and be unbound from them by the Word of the Lord.

My false belief in my call was that I would be alone in the unknown. As I bore this up to Jesus, the Refiner swiped away that slag with the truth that He would be with me. That removed my false belief based on sight and purified my faith that is anchored in His Word.

We pass some of those tests of faith and can look back, recount the blessings of obedience, and give thanks to God.

Some tests, we will fail—not on purpose, but because our faith in Jesus was mixed together with other things we trust. God can use failure to refine us and teach us to believe in the truth—just like he did for Peter who wrote the verse above on being tested in the fire.

Peter's Faith Refined

Peter believed in Jesus and followed Him, but he had another competing faith that needed to be uncovered and laid bare through testing. Peter didn't realize how much faith he placed in himself to follow Jesus.

He needed this exposed then sifted out of his heart. Then he could live in the supernatural strength and courage of Christ that would be required later in his calling.

Generally, men are culturally conditioned to be strong, brave, and bold. Peter had a great deal of this human strength. When Jesus and His disciples were confronted with those who came to arrest them, Peter drew his sword and cut off the ear of the servant of the high priest.

When our strength comes from us, it's corrupt and finite—incapable of achieving God's purposes. Only a purified faith in Jesus will bring us heroic courage and ability to discern the good, acceptable, and perfect will of God.

Later on that night, Peter was pressed and tested when he saw Jesus bound in the high priest's courtyard. God brought three people to question him about knowing Jesus.

We read Peter's reply to the third one: "Peter replied, 'Man, I don't know what you're talking about!' Just as he was speaking, the rooster crowed. The Lord turned and looked straight at Peter. Then Peter remembered the word the Lord had spoken to him: 'Before the rooster crows today, you will disown me three times.' And he went outside and wept bitterly" (Luke 22:60–62).

Jesus "looked straight at Peter." It's the face-to-face, eye-to-eye contact with the One he denied that struck Peter to the core. It broke him.

Tests are God's gracious way of exposing our self-trust. It's for our good and His glory. Then, and only then, can we be changed by God's grace. Though painful, Peter faced the One who loved him, in whom he believed, yet had just denied. He went out and wept bitterly.

That will be difficult for us, too, and we may feel like giving up. But later, Peter came to Jesus because he knew Jesus was gracious. He would not cast him out. That's what it took for Peter and that's what it will take for us.

We all have failures and can be purified in them if we respond like Peter and come to Jesus.

With this in mind, Matthew quotes Isaiah: "A bruised reed he will not break, and a smoldering wick he will not snuff out, till he has brought justice through to victory. In his name the nations will put their hope" (Matthew 12:20–21).

Bruised reeds and smoldering wicks are treated gently and graciously by Jesus. They are the ones who will be healed and given future assignments for His glory.

We must believe in the merciful nature of Jesus to grow in faith. We will need to come to Him broken more than once. The fire of failure is painful but purifying.

Peter's Restoration

Jesus came to the disciples by the sea after His resurrection. What did He say to the ones who had abandoned Him in His darkest hour? He cooked them breakfast and invited them over to eat with Him.

Then he called for Peter to walk with Him. As they walked, Jesus asked him the same probing question three times, "Peter, do you love me?" (See John 21:15–17.) The Scripture says, "Peter was hurt because he asked him the third time." Most likely, Peter remembered his three denials.

But the questions had a purpose. We have to face our failure…and learn from it. Jesus was calling Peter from the failure of pride to a purified belief and motive for service—love for Jesus.

Peter experienced a fire-forged faith in Jesus through the resolution of his failure. That purified motive would inspire Peter to stand in the strength of God and proclaim His gospel with great faith, courage, and confidence—even though persecuted.

Peter had been afraid of Caiaphas in the courtyard, but he would later be fearless in the courtyard of Caesar. He would give his all for love of the One who took it all for him.

Jesus had already prayed for Peter to prepare him for his test. He intercedes for all of us according to the will of God, just like he did for Peter.

Luke records, "'Simon, Simon, Satan has asked to sift all of you as wheat. But I have prayed for you, Simon, that your faith may not fail. And when you have turned back, strengthen your brothers'" (Luke 22:31–32).

The phrase, "But I have prayed for you…" is a powerful thought for anyone who is in a hard place right now. Maybe you need to receive this powerful truth that Jesus is interceding for you according to the will of the Father. Take great comfort in this fact. God is willing your good in the current circumstance that seems to be so difficult and impossible.

Sometimes, God uses Satan temporarily to advance His kingdom permanently. Peter's unbelief was known by God, but unknown by Peter until Satan sifted him. When this happens to us or the people we love, we can't see any good in it. We see only failure or injustice.

But redemption was on the mind of Jesus in His prayer for Peter. In this necessary test, Peter could no longer hide behind a façade of human strength. Jesus worked to purify Peter's faith and restore him to ministry. This purification had to happen for Peter to be readied for future service.

Our fears and anxiety can be the test that leads us to have our self-trust exposed and our faith in Jesus purified.

True courage and peace of mind do not come by human strength but by love for Jesus—a love that trusts. Peter was put on solid footing by the patience and kindness of God. The worldly chaff was separated from his godly faith, and that left Peter in a position to fulfill God's highest purpose for his life.

My Faith Refined and My Fear Dispelled

I really enjoyed ministry until someone got upset about something that I did or our church was doing. I would get very anxious about that. I would wake up at night fretting over how to proceed and keep people unified.

I felt stress during those times, though I didn't let on. I would try to win over the disaffected person. But trying to get someone to like you isn't a very righteous or peaceful way to live.

"What are people thinking?" My mind would worry over that question way too much. Why did I worry? Because I was afraid someone would disrupt all the good we had going. I feared I would lose everything I was working for if I had an enemy.

I honestly felt that you have to fear enemies—people that don't like you, are mad at you, or are just generally out of control. As hard as I tried, I could never win over everybody. There was always some person in my life that didn't particularly care for me no matter what I did.

I couldn't figure out why. It was out of my control. If they had any influence, I feared what they would do. I feared what they would say, and all the good going on at church was at risk in my mind.

I loved our people. They loved me. Most of the time, we had a wonderful sense of unity and peace. It was great—until someone threw me a curveball. Then I stressed out.

One day, someone in our church brought up the idea of being a host church for Celebrate Recovery (CR), a Christ-centered, twelve-step recovery program for anyone struggling with hurt, hang-ups, or addiction. I had heard that many people had life-changing experiences in CR. So, I enthusiastically agreed with the request, and we soon started.

I was pleased for our church to host CR in our building every Tuesday night. That is, until Dana told me she was going.

When she told me she was going to go for a hang-up she had, I knew I had to pray about going with her. I sure didn't want to. *I'm the pastor,* I thought. *I don't need to go. I can handle everything myself with the Lord.*

I prayed about it. The Lord said to go. So, I went.

I'm glad I did. We met in the worship center and sang worship songs led by our band. We heard some inspiring testimonies. Then we broke up into small groups.

After sharing a few ground rules, our small group leader shared his hang-up and why he got into CR. Then, he opened up the floor to see if anyone else wanted to share why they were there. He emphasized no one had to share, only those who were ready.

I was one of the few that went ahead and shared that first night. I told them that I was there to work on my anxiety about people. It felt good to get that off my chest and let everyone know that even the pastor was there to work on his stuff. No one thought less of me.

Over the next several weeks in CR, I took time to get to the root of my specific anxiety related to leading people. Participating in that small group helped me work through my emotions, talk about the nature of my anxiety, and reflect on where it might be coming from. I was taking this opportunity to identify what I believed and why I believed it.

Christ-centered recovery ministries help in many ways. First, you realize you are not alone. Second, you realize some people struggle with a lot more than you do. And most importantly, people listen as each one shares their story. That bonded us all together. We prayed for each other and pulled for each other. Jesus was working through it all.

After attending several sessions, I admitted that my sense of security was threatened by people who disagreed with me. It shouldn't be, but it was. Why did I feel threatened by them?

As I considered it, I began to realize that my mind associated these scenarios with being bullied or the fear of being bullied as a kid. I remembered a frightening event when one of my friends told me that a gang of older boys in another neighborhood hated the guys in our neighborhood. My friend said those boys "were going to ride their motorcycles up to where we lived and beat us up."

I swallowed it hook, line, and sinker.

To me, at age ten, that was traumatic. The only thing I really knew about those boys was that they were big and strong. I didn't know any of them personally, but I totally believed that report about those guys coming to beat us up.

I imagined it happening soon. I began watching out for their motorcycles. I couldn't sleep at night. I was on guard all the time. It gripped me with fear.

But it never happened.

As I thought through that experience, I began to ask myself, "What did you take in from that childhood threat? What lie did you adopt that caused your fear?" I searched my heart by following the emotion of fear, trying to discern what exactly it was that I feared.

I concluded that I had adopted the lie that "you must be afraid of people who don't like you because they will hurt you." That was my natural way of assessing reality. It was stuck in the back of my mind.

In my adult life, I couldn't just let that fear go and let people be people because I believed in my heart that I had something to guard against. I believed someone could sabotage my well-being, hurt me, and impact the good things we had going.

Wisdom, not fear, is to be our guide for decision-making. God leads with wisdom. Fear or any other negative emotion will cloud our ability to see the path God has for us to take. We will end up being our own worst enemy and sabotage God's blessings if fear motivates our actions and reactions to people.

We must overcome anxiety to fulfill God's plan. God is patient. He is working to help us overcome. But it was very important for me to take the time to work on overcoming a specific anxiety. Take the opportunities afforded you by God to join Him in this work to refine your faith.

I took the time for self-examination through CR. The group process helped. A lot of people stay in CR indefinitely or in other twelve-step groups to maintain their sobriety or emotional health. I affirm that.

But for me, it was an appointed season to understand what was going on inside of me, where it was coming from, and why I absorbed the deceitful lies. I realized all this and then there was a final step to take to freedom—a spiritual transaction to be made by the Holy Spirit and me.

Just like the walk Peter had with Jesus and the probing questions from Jesus about Peter's underlying motivations, I needed a Spirit-led talk with Jesus about the root cause of my anxious thoughts.

I laid these deceitful lies before Him, and He talked to me about it. Not verbally, but in a still small voice to bring His Word to my inmost being. God wants to do this for us because He loves us.

Paul writes about the way Jesus shows love for His own through what He does for them: "…just as Christ loved the church and gave himself up for her to make her holy, cleansing her by the washing with water through the word, and to present her to himself as a radiant church, without stain or wrinkle or any other blemish, but holy and blameless" (Ephesians 5:25–27).

Jesus expresses His love for His bride by cleansing her by the washing of His Word, dispelling false beliefs that keep us afraid or demoralized. His Word can wash those away one lie at a time.

So, I prayed, "Dear Lord, I feel those boys who don't like me are coming and will hurt me and damage my stuff. My false belief is that I have to be on guard with people who don't like me or I will get hurt."

After this confession, I opened myself up to listen to Jesus, and a truth came to my understanding: Jesus was with me; I didn't need to be afraid." I sensed His presence by my side. My heart calmed, and a deep trust in Jesus took over. I knew I was going to be all right no matter what happened. Why? Jesus was with me, and I knew it.

Then, a few other memories came to me about real bullies in my early life. There weren't many, but I took an inward look to see if I had taken in any other lie-based beliefs from my experiences. Then I submitted those lies up to Jesus and received the truths, "Do not fear. I love you. I am with you." I prayed in this way until all the fear was gone. My faith was refined by the revelation of God's Word in prayer.

More peace came to my life and ministry than I had ever had. More joy came, too. We really do have no one to fear.

David sang, "The LORD is my light and my salvation— whom shall I fear? The LORD is the stronghold of my life—of whom shall I be afraid. When the wicked advance against me to devour me, it is my enemies and my foes who will stumble and fall. Though an army besiege me, my heart will not fear; though war break out against me, even then I will be confident" (Psalm 27:1–3).

When our faith is refined, it gives us confidence to know God is for us. God spoke to Joshua before he and the nation of Israel crossed over Jordan to take possession of the Promised Land. "Have I not commanded you? Be strong and courageous. Do not be afraid; do not be discouraged, for the LORD your God will be with you wherever you go" (Joshua 1:9).

"God will be with you wherever you go" is a fear-destroying, anxiety-dispelling, worry-killing truth. We can position ourselves to receive this truth from the Lord.

When truth comes through prayer, it should always be consistent with the Word of God. If it's not, it's not from God. God takes the simplest, most basic truths from the Bible and plants them in our heart by His Spirit just where we need them. We just open up to Him and show him the hurt place and what we took in. He heals His bride with His Word and purifies our belief.

This purification of faith orders our belief system with the Word of God, the mind of Christ. Through the eyes of Jesus, no person is to be feared. And all are to be loved.

My Anxiety over Demons

"And having disarmed the powers and authorities, he made a public spectacle of them, triumphing over them by the cross" (Colossians 2:15).

In rural Kentucky, I found that people are more comfortable talking to their pastor about personal issues rather than driving an hour or more to see a counselor. It was a privilege for me to come alongside people, listen to their struggles, and pray with them. They knew I wouldn't judge them.

It wasn't long before someone told me they felt like their struggle was against a demon. They felt like it was a definite spiritual battle. When we prayed together, I could sense something different going on, and I felt anxiety about dealing with it.

We finished our session and scheduled another one in two weeks. I had a fear I needed to face to fulfill my calling.

About the same time, I had once again started running regularly. It was winter, so I had to run at night after work. I lived on a dead-end road on a lake. At the time, only one other house was occupied out our way.

I usually ran in the dark without a flashlight, so I was able to see only a faint outline of the road. I would run out to the main road and back, which took about thirty minutes.

Just before the end of the road was a small cemetery and an old, unused barn beside it. I liked the dark nights, but when I passed that cemetery and the wind rattled a loose piece of the tin roof, I got really anxious and picked up my pace.

I kept telling myself there was nothing to it. I logically knew what was going on. The wind was banging those loose tin sheets together. But it scared me to death. Why? Where was my faith?

Well, that is the question I had to answer to be free. So, the next time I ran, I was ready. When I got to that old barn and cemetery on a pitch-black night, the tin roof clanged, and the fear automatically kicked in, even though I was ready for it.

I was too afraid to stop and pray. I ran away from that cemetery so fast I could have medaled at the Olympics. After I got home and settled down, I knew that my mind had associated the scene with two things.

First was my irrational fear when I was a little boy of being afraid to go up to our second-floor attic alone because of the monsters that lived up there. I would be so frightened by the thought of that old attic with all of the old furniture, bookshelves, a wardrobe, old clothes, and two big cut-out holes in our wall.

It was a nightmare for a little boy, knowing just how many places a monster could be hiding. It happened in my dreams, too. Monsters were real to me back then.

The second memory was from spending the night with one of my elementary school friends. My friend said that his father told ghost stories that were real...not made up. We pleaded with his dad until he relented and told us a couple.

The one I remember the most vividly occurred in a cemetery where the ghost of a man who had been unjustly killed came out at night. He carried a dimly lit lantern that creaked when he walked through the cemetery. He came out every night looking to avenge his wrongful death. This experience of a story told to me as true stuck in my mind.

Though I was an adult, my mind was associating demons with the ghosts and monsters in my memories. I knew there were no ghosts or monsters, but there are demons. They were the hidden bad actors. That's why I was afraid of the demons.

I would have nightmares of having to face a demon in the attic or in a counseling session. In my dreams, I would inevitably face a demon and try to drive it away by saying, "In Jesus' name, I rebuke you! Be gone!" But I couldn't get the words out because I was so frightened. I would wake up sweating and so relieved I wasn't actually facing a demon.

I had to overcome this anxiety. I knew the Scriptures. I rehearsed my authority over demons in Christ. I prayed and thought that I had the courage and confidence I needed. Then, the thought of facing one in a prayer session would frighten me.

I started to realize I was just fooling myself, trying to "drum up" the nerve to be confident. When the chips are down, acting like you are not afraid won't cut it. We need to *be not* afraid, not *act* like we are not afraid.

I knew I couldn't just act like a confident Christian pastor because the demons would know. Remember the seven sons of Sceva in Acts 19:11–20?

No matter how many Bible verses I memorized, it didn't help this anxiety. I needed to go to the root of the problem and unlearn something that was still stuck in my belief system.

The Spirit of Christ would unbind me from the lies. I simply needed to get myself in a position to receive ministry from Him. For most things, that means getting real, opening up, and confessing what we believe that's false in the situation and why we believe it.

My mind associated demons with the ghosts and monsters that I had feared but could not see as a child. They were the unseen enemy. I couldn't prevent that association from happening. It was automatic.

When people who don't struggle with our specific anxiety find out we fear something, they may say, "There is nothing to fear" or "Just get over it." It's easy for people to say that, but it doesn't help. No one wants to be anxious. We are not willing ourselves to have anxiety. Our faith needs to be refined.

When I got home from running that night, I got alone with God and prayed. I went back to the first memory and confessed, "Lord, I am afraid of the monster-like demons up in the attic because they are real and want to kill me. Please show me the truth."

In a few seconds, I discerned the truth that Jesus was right there with me, and He is more powerful than demons." My fears calmed as I realized this. The light came on in my understanding by the illumination of the Holy Spirit. God is with me, and God is greater than any demon.

In the second memory, I confessed, "Lord, I fear demons like the ghosts in this story. I believe they have power over me and want to harm me."

I offered that up to Jesus, and in a moment, the truth came to me. "God is with me, He has disarmed the demons, and they have no power over me because I am His." I slowly took that in.

Peace filled my soul as Jesus imparted biblical truth just where I needed it. The Word of God is the Sword of the Spirit who cuts away our lie-based beliefs with the truth. My faith was refined by God's living Word.

It wasn't long before the person who had a spiritual battle going on returned to my office. As we talked it through, she told me she had remembered dabbling in an occult practice as a teenager.

A week before, I would have felt anxiety over this revelation. But now, in peace and confidence, I lead her to renounce the sin of this particular ritual in prayer. She did. Then I asked Jesus to show her the truth.

The truth came to her understanding that the ritual was wrong, and God loved her and forgave her. The darkness lifted. She was free. Demons can't possess a believer, but they can get a foothold in our lives if we have allowed it.

We all need to face our fears and have our faith refined so that we sense God present and at work. Our naturalistic or superstitious way of viewing life and assessing situations can be informed by a renewed understanding of the Word that will always result in peace.

Questions for Reflection and Application

1. Peter's faith was refined through his failure. Describe a recent failure that caused you distress.

    a. In hindsight, what were you putting your faith in during that failure? What can you learn from it?

    b. Consider how Jesus treated Peter after his failure. If Jesus called you to His side to walk along the shore, what do you feel He would say to you to refine your faith and restore you?

    c. Write out your talk with Jesus. Listen to His voice. Consider His Word.

    d. When you are ready, let the failure go and move forward with what Jesus has said to you.

2. "Lord, I do believe: help me overcome my unbelief" (Mark 9:24). Are you facing something beyond your ability to fix? Describe how it makes you feel?

    a. Underneath the surface of your feelings, what is your heart trusting in that is mingled with your faith in God?

    b. Write out a prayer asking God to refine your faith in the crucible of this trial.

3. Describe the situation you are dealing with now that causes you to have anxious thoughts.

Refine Your Faith

a. Does a related situation come to your mind that may be the root cause?

b. What was that situation?

c. How does it feel similar?

d. What did you take in from that experience?

e. Do you feel like the enemy planted a lie in your mind that stuck with you? What is that lie or lies?

f. Submit those lies to Jesus. "Lord Jesus, this is what I took in from that experience." Name the lies. Then say, "Lord Jesus, please show me the truth."

g. Listen for His reply.

h. Write out what Jesus says.

Chapter 7

Process Your Emotions

"While he was still speaking, yet another messenger came and said, 'Your sons and daughters were feasting and drinking wine at the oldest brother's house, when suddenly a mighty wind swept in from the desert and struck the four corners of the house. It collapsed on them and they are dead, and I am the only one who has escaped to tell you!'"

JOB 1:18–19

Divorce, loss of a job, losing a loved one, trauma, a cancer diagnosis...these are the kinds of unexpected life events that rock our world and shock our system. They can shake us and knock us off our foundation. We will naturally feel anxiety for a while until we find our footing again. That's normal and necessary.

Events like these can trigger anxiety over things we never gave a thought to before. In gentleness and love, Jesus is there to shepherd us through the darkest valleys. He wants us to connect with Him in our hardship and process our thoughts and emotions to a deeper life of faith.

It could take a few minutes or a few months, depending on the nature of the event, our readiness to change, or our openness to transparency. When we face devastating news, God will help us, but we must open up and be really honest with Him. Then peace will come.

Fear of Death

The fear of death is a huge issue that can surface during a landmark event in life. We avoid thinking about it, but this fear underlies a lot of our specific anxieties. A big jolt to our everyday life by an unforeseen incident can trigger this fear that we had previously been able to avoid. During those times, we must face our mortality.

Death is a fundamental fear. We are powerless over it. No one is exempt, no matter their status in life. People try to cope with it in different ways but avoidance seems to be the most common—out of sight, out of mind. There is little anxiety over death—until it surfaces in an unanticipated life event.

We need to face our own mortality. Even Christians who walk with God have to face this prospect and sometimes feel tremendous anxiety.

In the natural realm, nothing tests our sense of personal security more than death. When confronted with it, we must look into the void and ask ourselves the ultimate question: "What is going to happen to me after I die?" This is the fundamental question.

John Owen wrote, "We cannot enjoy peace in this world unless we are ready to yield to the will of God in respect of death. Our times are in His hand, at His sovereign disposal. We must accept that as best."[7]

One weekend, my friend, Ron Minnix, was at home and felt the symptoms of a heart attack. Ron worked as a supervisor of commercial construction projects and was very active. At first, he couldn't imagine that he was having a heart attack though the pain in his chest was acute. His wife, Janice, called 911.

The paramedics arrived and told Ron he needed to go to the hospital immediately. They put him on a gurney and wheeled him outside toward the ambulance.

Ron knew then that he could die at any moment. He felt very anxious. Ron described what happened next, "I looked up in the sky and prayed, 'It's in your hands, Lord. Let it be.'" Then he said, "A calm came over me that I can't explain other than God gave me peace. I knew it was in His hands."

Ron didn't try to come up with the right language to use in his prayer. He didn't use a lot of words. But he did call out to God with helpless desperation straight from the heart. Ron got real with God and spoke to Him from the depths of his soul.

---

[7] John Owen, *Meditation on the Glory of Christ,* (Grand Rapids, MI: Christian Classics Ethereal Library, 2010), Preface.

The need for honesty and transparency is crucial to get traction with God. It's like a car on a rack. We can push the pedal to the metal, the engine will sound off, but the car will go nowhere. The rubber has to meet the road to get the traction it needs. Transparent honesty gets traction with God. His kingdom moves on it.

When unfiltered reality is expressed to God, then Ultimate Reality expresses Himself back to you. It's called the voice of God. That voice is powerful and effective. Jesus gave Ron His peace.

For the Jews in the Bible, "calling out to God" came from the gut—the very core of a person. In traumatic times, it is desperately needed. It doesn't matter as much *what* you pray, but *where* you pray from.

An honest prayer from a discouraged believer in Psalm 42 says, "Deep calls to deep in the roar of your waterfalls; all your waves and breakers have swept over me" (Psalm 42:7).

When God permits the waves of life to sweep over you and discourage you, "deep will be calling to deep" to take you to the depths of His love and power. That deep place can only be experienced in helplessness. Letting go and taking a deep dive into the depths of God's presence by faith will strike a mortal blow to your anxiety.

Several years after Ron's heart attack, he needed another surgery. I visited him in his hospital room before this surgery and asked him how he felt about it. He replied, "I see this as a win-win situation. If I make it through, it's more time to serve God and be with my family. If not, God calls me home to heaven to be with Jesus. Either way, it's a win."

Through Ron's previous encounter with the prospect of dying, his faith had been formed and was still there giving Him peace and guarding his heart for this surgery. But this time, God took Ron home a few days later. His faith gave him the ultimate healing, the ultimate victory. It was Ron's biggest win by far.

That wasn't the only win for my friend. His family had been deeply affected by their dad or granddad's faith and confidence in the face of death. Their faith has been strengthened by his testimony. Ron gave them a template on how to face life's biggest challenges. What a gift to leave your family.

Ron's daughter had his prayer tattooed on her arm: "It's in your hands, Lord. Let it be." It's a reminder for her to pray and trust God when life presses in.

Jesus calls us to overcome the world through Him. It doesn't mean we don't struggle or suffer. Big challenges like death will come that are beyond our finite capacity to bear alone. We will fear, but our faith will not fail.

Faith has to form to meet the particular challenge we face. Once it does, peace soon follows and will guard your heart. God has willed us to face the overwhelming flood of this world. But He will impart His overcoming grace to us for the eternal glory of His name when we practice our faith.

As a pastor, I visited many hospitals and prayed with people before major surgeries. I would often ask, "How are you feeling about everything?" I wanted to give people a chance to process whatever was on their mind and then pray about it with them. Often, they would share with me how they had already talked to Jesus about the surgery and had peace. Some were not completely at peace yet.

After they shared their feelings, I would ask them if they were ready to put this surgery and their life in God's hands. They would answer "yes," and I would pray with them something like:

"Jesus, we put this surgery in Your hands and trust You to bless and use the doctors and medical team to bring the help we need. We put our life in Your hands, Lord, and yield completely to You."

Often, this process resulted in the peace of Christ.

If we don't deal with our fear of death by facing it, processing it, and praying through it, we will be under the influence of fear the rest of our lives. It will come out in various decisions, raising kids, keeping grandkids...and it may negatively influence others and cause them to fear.

We mean them no harm; quite to the contrary, we want to keep ourselves and the kids safe. But fear will seep out of our minds and into our voice and decisions and affect our world.

Anxiety can linger and last longer than the unexpected life event, and we can get stuck in unhealthy patterns of thinking. The unhealthy train of thought must be broken so we can move forward and find new life and peace in our new normal. Processing to get to the change is necessary.

The Purpose in Processing

When overcome with a crisis of faith, we need to process what happened to us so new mental pathways of hope and peace can form. We have to work through our troublesome thoughts, not avoid them.

Avoidance will just pack away our pain. It will imbed in our soul and seep into our emotions—even our physical health can be affected. We do not want to carry something like baggage when God can unburden us.

The ultimate goal of processing is to know God's comfort and come into the strong hope and security that we have in Christ. In processing, we are not ruminating on the past but working through the painful to get to the peaceful. Endless talk is not going to create a pathway to peace, but processing with this purpose absolutely can.

We can access God's help to form new pathways of viewing reality through expressing our thoughts and fears. With the Holy Spirit guiding you, you share your present thoughts and feelings with God who can lead you to form a new mental outlook in the light of His Word.

The goal is to go from *our* understanding of the situation to *God's view* of the situation. It's a process with a purpose.

Reflecting on what we feel internally and expressing the emotions associated with it is crucial. The Psalms are filled with King David and others processing their thoughts and emotions with God. Often, they went from processing to praise, from confession to thanksgiving, from thoughts of defeat to believing in victory.

That's the goal—to bring our thoughts, beliefs, feelings, and actions into alignment with God and His will. That's why we must process intentionally to that end. It is highly effective.

Process with Children

Kids go through challenging times at school, on the playground, at sleepovers or birthday parties, in sports, while playing with cousins...Parents need to process with their children so they don't get stuck with a lie-based view of certain situations.

Of course, kids don't need to be interrogated after every event. Just remember to ask, "How did it go?" then read your kids.

I've noticed that a lot of parents can read their kids pretty well. If they get a one-word answer from their big talker, they know something is up. That's when your discernment as a parent kicks in. Do they have something they need to tell you?

Maybe later on, you can ask them, "Did anything happen at the party that made you feel uncomfortable?" Kids need to process their day with an adult who can help them come to the truth before it gets stuck inside.

We all remember how stuff happens when it's just kids around or there is an unscrupulous adult present. Asking good questions that help children open up if they are feeling afraid is important. You can help them process from fear to a healthy view of what people have said or done. If it's been an emotionally tough day, you will be able to help them work through it.

Praying before bedtime is an excellent habit to develop early on. It's a way to release it all to God and get back to thinking good thoughts and feeling at peace before bedtime. If you and your teen don't do that anymore, you may be able to return to this practice during difficult times.

Process with Your Spouse

Last year, we moved to Minnesota to be close to Dana's parents. Her dad has Alzheimer's disease. He has declined in his ability to function as the disease has progressed. It's hard. You lose your family member one piece at a time. That's a lot of grieving.

You need to grieve one loss at a time. Dana is with her parents for some time most everyday helping out as needed. About once a week, she has to work through grieving the loss of another part of her dad.

When that moment comes for Dana to grieve, I sit with her while she talks. I may ask an open-ended question like, "How is it going for your dad? How does that make you feel?" "How about your mom, how is she holding up?"

But mainly, I empathize and listen. After talk and tears, Dana transitions to prayer. I join her in spirit and presence. After Dana prays, she is at peace and ready to continue her journey.

We are our spouse's helpmate. Providing emotional support is crucial to getting through life's challenges together. Asking our spouse how we can best "be there" for them will make a huge difference. From experience, here are a few tips I have learned for everyone, especially husbands.

1. Don't try to solve her problem. Listen to her heart.
2. Give her your full attention the whole time.
3. Accept her and her tears. It's part of the healing process.
4. Don't give her advice unless she asks for it.
5. Be the one she can talk to.

Give her this gift, my friend, and you will be blessed. She just needs you to be there for her—fully present. If she has a meltdown, don't get nervous. Everything is going to be okay. It's a good thing. She will figure it out through this and peace will come. She needs a trusted friend she can talk to who will listen to her. Be that friend.

You probably won't need to process like this often, but there will definitely be moments when you need to take a page out of her playbook and open up just like her. Don't deny stuff, hide it, stuff it, or silently suffer with it. She is there for you. Let her be that person for you.

Intimacy is formed through knowing on all levels—including emotional and spiritual. Knowing each other in this way bonds you together in Christ who knows you best—process with her and Jesus. Open up and let her know what you are dealing with. Pray together, and God will draw you close.

Process with God

Learning to process with God is crucial for all of us. Not everyone is comfortable with it or knows exactly how to go about it. But it is important to learn how in order to come to peace. My biggest advice on how to do this is to get alone, let go, and pour out your thoughts and emotions to God.

Do not lie or put on with God. Tell Him how you feel and what you are thinking. Do not hold back. Make this your practice, and you will learn how to have peace in any situation.

Read how warrior David processed with God in a cave while fleeing King Saul: "I cry out to God Most High, to God, who vindicates me. He sends from heaven and saves me, rebuking those who hotly pursue me—God sends forth his love and his faithfulness. I am in the midst of lions; I am forced to dwell among ravenous beasts—men whose teeth are spears and arrows, whose tongues are sharp swords" (Psalm 57:2–4).

David's life was on the line. He and his friends were vastly outnumbered. He needed mercy and assurance. David expresses his feelings and why he feels the way he does in prayer. By the time He gets to the end of this processing Psalm, a new mental pathway for viewing the situation has formed in David's understanding.

He continues: "I will praise you, Lord, among the nations; I will sing of you among the peoples. For great is your love, reaching to the heavens; your faithfulness reaches to the skies. Be exalted, O God, above the heavens; let your glory be over all the earth" (Psalm 57:9–11).

David went from seeing sharp swords in the field to seeing the faithfulness of God in the skies. Processing with God during a crisis can enable your mind to come into the light of the truth in any cave. It results in an unshakeable confidence in God.

Processing in prayer is to be an integral part of our response to the crises of our lives. It is the practice described in the New Testament in I Peter 5:7, which says, "Cast all your anxiety on Him, because He cares for you."

We cast anxiety out of our soul by crying out to God in prayer. Then He casts back His peace. It's a great exchange and a great promise.

To "cry out" to God means to express a desperate plea for God's mercy with deep feeling and emotion. It is a cry of personal helplessness, yet at the same time, personal trust in God's love and power. Please take advantage of this powerful prayer that unburdens the soul.

We need to get over feeling like it is a childish thing to do. There is a difference between *childlike* and *childish*. Childlike virtues are to be practiced, and childish selfishness is to be shunned. This practice is a godly way to connect with Jesus during our stress-filled trials and find His peace.

Just get alone with God and offer up your worries to Him in prayer. Trust Him. Then listen to God and receive His help.

Hebrews 5:7 describes how the Ultimate Man processed His painful trials: "During the days of Jesus' life on earth, he offered up prayers and petitions with fervent cries and tears to the one who could save him from death, and he was heard because of his reverent submission."

Jesus was being fully human and genuinely praying to His Father during the days of His life on earth. He went before us to show us how to live and pray.

At crucial times in our lives, we will need to pray in such a way that will restore peace to our souls. F.B. Meyer wrote, "As we pour out our bitterness, God pours in his peace."[8]

---

[8] F.B. Meyer, *F.B. Meyer Quotes,* www.goodreads.com.

The cry of the heart draws down the consolations of heaven like the cry of a child draws the help of a parent. Our heavenly Father will give us the help we need—comfort, guidance, and assurance.

Processing My Financial Fear with God

Southern Baptist pastors don't have pensions like some centralized denominations. So, we pastors pay social security taxes to the government, but beyond that, it's up to the individual minister to save.

Thankfully, early on, a minister friend encouraged me to invest in a 403b retirement account. I reluctantly did so and over the years, like most stock mutual funds, the value increased. It was a wise decision.

But this wise decision and good investment morphed into my security blanket. Sometimes our blessings can become our idols.

When the stock market didn't behave like I anticipated, it caused me a lot of worry. I needed to process and get to the bottom of it—not to complain or gripe—but to be transformed and become like Jesus. I followed the fear back to the root source of my insecurity. The memory was etched into my mind from the age of twelve.

I was on a golf course practicing putting just outside our clubhouse when I looked up and saw Mrs. McVey, our Junior Golf leader and close family friend, walking toward me. She seemed to be very sad.

I asked, "What's wrong, Mrs. McVey? Did I not win my age group after all?" She said, "Jake, your father has died." I immediately dropped to the ground in uncontrollable grief.

He had been in the hospital, but I had point blank asked my mom if he was going to die, and she had said no. I don't think anyone thought he was going to die.

This unexpected news knocked the floor out from underneath my life. Along with the initial heart-wrenching grief over my dad's sudden loss, the thoughts going through my head were, "What is going to happen to us now? How are we going to make it? How are we going to get money to live?" I never really got a good answer to those questions. I didn't process it with anyone.

These questions were seared into my consciousness and were triggered later in life when anything suddenly threatened my security. Events like changes in the stock market would set my heart racing, my mind calculating, and my anxiety level escalating. That life event of suddenly and unexpectedly losing my dad, my security blanket, left me with financial insecurities.

I had to face this event and process it with Jesus, the Wonderful Counselor, until I found peace in the particular event that triggered my financial anxiety. After much soul searching, I identified the lies I had absorbed through Dad's shocking death—"We are all alone, doom is just around the corner, there will not be enough money."

I submitted these lies up to the Lord and invited Jesus to show me the truth. "You are not alone, I am in control, and you can trust Me to care for you" eventually came to my understanding. God changed my view of security. His truth replaced the lies and brought me into one accord with the Word of God.

Now, when the stock market jitters, I don't. Up or down, God is in control, and He will be there for me when the day is done.

You might be someone like me who did not process some difficult life event very well. I just moved on, but later on, I had to come back to it because it wasn't resolved. I kept experiencing anxiety over finances and the future. Resolution comes through processing under the leadership of the Holy Spirit that forms a new pathway of viewing our life.

I also had a lot of unexpressed grief. It was good to finally work through it. I also had some things left unsaid to my dad who had abruptly passed away. I talked to God about it. It was a blessing for my soul.

If we open up, process what troubles us, and listen to God, His peace will form.

Process with People You Trust

If you have a friendship with a fellow believer (of the same sex) and you genuinely listen while the other person processes life's challenges, then you have a tremendous resource for peace.

If you can pray with each other about such matters, then you will also have Jesus in your midst to impart His Word to you. Prayer takes it to another level. This combination is a great way to grow through life's challenges. "For where two or three gather in my name, there am I with them" (Matthew 18:20).

Keep in mind again that processing is not just venting or complaining. The time spent with a trusted friend is to share where you are mentally and emotionally—your true thoughts and feelings—in order to cross a divinely-built bridge to the mind of Christ, a new way of thinking.

Hearing yourself articulate your current thoughts and emotions will help you come to terms with what is going on inside of you. This facilitates the change we need.

The following verse is a template for healing. James writes, "Therefore confess your sins to each other and pray for each other so that you may be healed. The prayer of a righteous person is powerful and effective" (James 5:16).

Finding a good pastor, Christian counselor, or therapist to open up to and be transparent with is a good option for many when working through excessive anxiety or worry.

Some churches also have a Stephen Ministry that trains trusted laypeople to come alongside people and walk with them through a hard time. These trained ministers are able to ask good questions that can help you discern what's going on inside of you. View it as going to see someone who is there to help you look under your own hood to identify and work through a problem with God's help.

You can diagnose through processing, but healing comes through prayer and the Word. You may not have time to pray in a counseling session that lasts just one hour, but you need to make time to pray either by yourself, with a friend, or minister.

Process with Pen

When God called me to Africa for a two-year mission assignment, I was twenty-five years old and had never been out of the country. Our training by the International Mission Board suggested prayer journaling as a way to transition to a new culture.

I knew this big transition would put me into challenging circumstances that carried with them the potential for overwhelming anxiety. I decided to journal as a regular discipline for the first few weeks.

At the end of each day, I wrote down my thoughts and feelings as if I were writing a letter home to God. This proved to be a blessing as I prayed through with a pen everything I was experiencing as new.

As I wrote, Scriptures often came to mind. They intersected my life in those moments and put light on my path. This processing helped my mental transition to a new country and culture. That was the goal of my processing with pen.

After a few months, I stopped. I had mentally and emotionally arrived where I needed to be, with peace and confidence to live and work in a new environment. I had adjusted. My new thought processes developed faster and more thoroughly with prayer journaling.

Journaling has tremendous potential to take us from old pathways of thinking into new ones that reflect God's truth. Write your true thoughts and emotions in a journal to God. Then reflect on the Scriptures God gives you and write those down. This two-way communication facilitates coming into a new understanding of your circumstances.

Sometimes, writing a letter to a person can bring you to peace or closure. It may be a person who passed away before you had a chance to tell them all you wanted or needed to say. Or perhaps someone has offended you, and you write to them, stating exactly how you feel about what happened.

Then you can pray. Afterwards, God will give you peace and wisdom regarding how to proceed. Many people throw away the letter and start anew in their approach as God gives direction. Clarity comes after we process to peace.

A Christ-Centered Support Group

Support groups are an excellent choice to help people work through what happened or what's going on inside. As I shared earlier, Celebrate Recovery helped me identify the lie-based belief causing my anxiety. Then, I could express this to

God and come under the influence of the Holy Spirit in prayer that set me free from that particular anxiety.

Many different kinds of groups are geared toward helping people who share a common struggle—divorce recovery, abuse recovery, grief support. In these gatherings, people come together with a trained facilitator and some good material to promote growth in Christ. Sharing is encouraged but optional.

Each person proceeds at his or her own pace. The presence of a trained facilitator and Bible-based material gives much-needed focus. Everyone has the opportunity to experience Christ in community with others.

The fellowship is a powerful dynamic because we can take comfort from others who know how we feel. Sharing the journey with fellow strugglers can be the bridge you need to a better tomorrow. The Presence of Christ will be manifested through love, the Word, prayer, and the spiritual gifts of the participants.

The Fruit of Processing

The goal of talking through our struggles is to bring our whole being—body, mind, faith, and actions—in line with God's Word. A deeper revelation of God's love, holiness, and power will transform our mental state.

"But the seed falling on good soil refers to someone who hears the word and understands it. This is the one who produces a crop, yielding a hundred, sixty or thirty times what was sown" (Matthew 13:23).

The Word of God can sink into those deep places within us as we open up to God with a desire to understand and be changed. The Living Word implanted into our soul effects godly change and healthy emotions. When this happens, there is no going back. The change in that particular place in our mind is permanent.

That's why I don't have to "get prayed up" or "get my mind right" before getting on a flight. The victory is effortless now. The hard work is over. The ground was plowed, the seed was sown, and the harvest of righteousness came. Process and pray. Be patient. Persevere. Peace will form as your faith is refined.

A Processing Prophet

The story of Elisha the prophet contains a famous scene when he helped his anxious servant process to faith and peace.

Elisha was in the city of Dothan, and the King of Syria sent a great army to besiege the city and kill Elisha. Elisha, who is referred to as "the man of God," had a servant who came out to be with him in the field as the army approached. The servant was naturally afraid.

Read how Elisha helped him. "When the servant of the man of God got up and went out early the next morning, an army with horses and chariots had surrounded the city. 'Oh no, my lord! What shall we do?' the servant asked.

'Don't be afraid,' the prophet answered. 'Those who are with us are more than those who are with them.' And Elisha prayed, 'Open his eyes, LORD, so that he may see.' Then the LORD opened the servant's eyes, and he looked and saw the hills full of horses and chariots of fire all around Elisha" (II Kings 6:15–17).

The natural man sees only the physical realities around him. But the spiritual man perceives a greater spiritual truth in the midst of the situation that brings peace and assurance. We are like Elisha's servant when we view our threatening situation with great fear. We see only the threat.

While Elisha's servant believed in God and loved the man of God, he understandably didn't have the faith of Elisha—yet. Elisha had the tremendous privilege of being Elijah's disciple for years. His faith formed while following his mentor Elijah as he saw and experienced the great things God did.

Elisha listened to his servant's fearful and desperate words and said afterwards, "Do not be afraid." Then he prayed for him with the expectation that God would move in the servant's life to reveal the truth.

God opened the servant's eyes, and he saw the chariots of fire all around them. When this revelation of truth came, the fear went away.

We should not think we are any different. We are all on this journey of growing in faith. Processing will help facilitate our coming into a greater faith in the unseen realities of the kingdom of God. Courage and peace will then be ours in abundance.

Questions for Reflection and Application

1. What is the purpose in processing? Why is it so important in overcoming our anxiety?

2. Remember a time when you processed your thoughts and feelings and crossed a bridge to a brighter outlook? Who did you process with? How did that help you?

3. Have you ever had to face your own mortality? If so, how did you process it? Do you have any leftover fear about death?

4. How can you improve in helping other people process their thoughts and emotions—your children, spouse, or friends?

5. Is God leading you to consider processing your fears and anxieties in a Christian support group or with a trained pastor or Christian counselor? Write out a prayer asking God to show you the way to get the help you need.

Chapter 8

Center Your Heart

"Whoever dwells in the shelter of the Most High will rest in the shadow of the Almighty. I will say of the LORD, 'He is my refuge and my fortress, my God, in whom I trust.'"

- PSALM 91:1–2

G od is our safe place. He is our shelter in the storm, our refuge in the night, and our fortress in the battle. To dwell in conscious awareness of God's presence is to dwell in peace. He is our secret place of security.

The Lord is our spiritual home. It's where we belong. Our mind is put at ease there. There is no safer or sweeter place to be than in His presence. God is our sanctuary.

We are to live in Christ, abide in Him. Anxiety and stress can't survive under the shadow of the Almighty. Our soul can relax and be relieved of tension in the shelter of the Most High. Where is that shelter? He is with you right now.

Jesus tells us, "Anyone who loves me will obey my teaching. My Father will love them, and we will come to them and make our home with them" (John 14:23).

Jesus and the Father have come and made their home with you. They live with you. That's why we don't need to be troubled about anything.

When we are at home, we are at peace, comfortable, and at ease. The Triune God has made His home with every true believer—our home is God Himself.

We often think of our home with God in heaven, and we should. But God didn't wait. Jesus and the Father have made their home with us on earth right now. Take some time and let that peace-giving truth sink in.

God will always be with you wherever you go and whatever you do. When you can perceive Him by your side, you will experience peace regardless of where you are physically—whether you are in a prison like Paul or on a vacation by the sea. When your heart is in its rightful place, your mind will be at ease.

Live Inside Your Home

Not being aware of the abiding presence of God is like getting home at night from a long day at work but not going inside your house to enjoy its light, comfort, and safety.

The next time you come home from somewhere, imagine what it would be like not to go in your house—just take a seat on the lawn. Feel what it's like.

Cooking, sitting, and sleeping outside in the elements is stressful. You realize how vulnerable you are at night when you are living without a shelter. We forfeit peace and comfort and much more when we are not consciously abiding in God's presence.

We are meant to live in Christ and enjoy the security He gives. Our spiritual home is bigger than any problem and more compelling than any person. God's voice can calm any storm. His gentle touch can reassure every heart. His food is the best, and His water is the sweetest.

Our problem is that we don't often realize what we have. If Christians were asked, "Where do you live?" how many of us would say "in Christ." To most of us, our physical home would come to mind. It's nice to have it.

But our heart has a home too, a spiritual dwelling place. It's the Most High God. And we won't rest until we abide there with Him. Instead, we will continue to live in our thoughts with stress and fear.

Augustine wrote, "You have formed us for yourself, and our hearts are restless till they find their rest in you."

Lean into the Arms of God

Home is where the heart is, so we need a settled intention to center our heart in Jesus and dwell in His shelter. There, your mind can be calm and your weary heart can feel the comfort of His embrace. "The eternal God is your refuge, and underneath are the everlasting arms" (Deuteronomy 33:27).

You can lean into God's everlasting arms, be loved, and know everything will be all right. While you rest in Him, God will be at work in you restoring your soul and enlivening your spirit.

Anxiety and stress flow out when you enter your dwelling. It's impossible for those two emotions to set foot in that holy place. They will always leave you there with God.

God is a beautiful home abounding in spiritual riches and pure pleasures. In Him, our deepest longings are satisfied and our greatest desires are fulfilled. This place has the best friend you can ever imagine living there with you. He calls you by name, and He calls you His friend.

Because we can't see this place, we don't think it's as important to our well-being as our physical dwelling. But the spiritual reality that God Himself is our dwelling place is more real than any physical home ever built.

His Presence is more powerful than any physical threat that is comprehended by sight. We are to learn to live in Him and have peace, "for in him we live and move and have our being" (Acts 17:28).

How do we increase our faith to know His presence more? I don't think that is the right question because the faith of a small mustard seed can move a mountain.

What we must do is apply the faith we have been given. We must take it off the shelf during our normal day and put it into practice.

Through the following practices, you can center your heart in Jesus, become more aware of His Presence, and live in His peace. He will gladly make Himself known to anyone who seeks Him.

Practice the Presence of God

Practices that increase our awareness of God throughout our day start with the mind then travel to the heart. Isaiah wrote a compelling truth: "You keep him in perfect peace whose mind is stayed on you, because he trusts in you" (Isaiah 26:3, ESV).

The verse above is a powerful daily promise available to all. If we can train our mind to stay upon Jesus and our heart to trust in Him, He will give us not just any kind of peace— but perfect peace.

The spiritual practices in this section will help you to grow a more God-focused life that is profoundly satisfying. This focus produces worriless calm, a restful assurance, and a humble confidence that everything is going to work out no matter what happens.

The following habits are not to be taken as a legalistic way of living. We don't live by rules, but through love. In one of His prayers to the Father, we learn, "Now this is eternal life: that they know you, the only true God, and Jesus Christ, whom you have sent" (John 17:3).

Eternal life is to know God and know Jesus. He is to be the center of our existence both now and forevermore. That's why the title of this chapter is "Center Your Heart." Knowing God is ultimate. He created us for a love relationship.

A.W. Tozer wrote, "God formed us for His pleasure, and so formed us that we as well as He can in divine communion enjoy the sweet and mysterious mingling of kindred personalities. He meant us to see Him and live with Him and draw our life from His smile."[9]

These spiritual practices will help you achieve your goal to enjoy sweet communion with Jesus and "draw life from His smile." Being aware of His company will give you a tranquil heart and so much more.

Prayer

Each practice affects the others. A heart that has been broken through confessions and repentance can be saturated with God in prayer. A heart of flesh, like a sponge, is able to soak in His presence. Take advantage of this blessed state of your heart and practice prayer.

If you are just beginning or trying to reboot your spiritual life, start out small. When someone goes from being a couch potato to a marathoner, they begin with walking not running. So, start small, then stick with it no matter how you feel.

---

9 A. W. Tozer, The Pursuit of God, E-book, (Abbotsford, WI: Aneko Press, 2015, First edition published 1948, Christian Publications, Harrisburg, PA), 17.

Someone has said, "The only way you can fail at prayer is to fail to pray." Fair weather walkers and runners are not going to get very far in their marathon training. It takes consistency. Focus on developing the habit. Then you can add more as you grow. In fact, you will desire that.

Prayer is a relationship first. That's why the model prayer begins with, "Our Father." Think about this relationship with your good, good Father. Try to savor that in your soul. It's special, like no other. Our Father takes great delight in His children and wants us to know Him.

Our Father has made His home with us. Enjoy Him. God's first desire for you in prayer is to know Him.

We are to draw life from this relationship and live from it. In our natural state, we live through our mind—toiling, figuring, and fretting. Our unredeemed mind spins like a top and, by centrifugal force, draws our life up into our mind.

But now we have Jesus. We have life. Quiet times, prayers of love and trust, slow our mind. Then we sink into our regenerated heart and commune with God.

Slow down and let this calm to come to your soul. "He makes me lie down in green pastures. He leads me beside still waters. He restores my soul" (Psalm 23:2–3, ESV).

That's first on our Good Shepherd's agenda. Before we walk in paths of righteousness, we rest in green pastures with Jesus.

Good Prayer Habits

At the start of every day, we can get on our knees before the King of the Universe and recognize who He is. In the morning, I microwave my tea, get one of Dana's decorative pillows (don't tell), put it on the floor by the couch, get down on my knees, and acknowledge Jesus is Lord over all. I put myself under His rule.

After I am fully submitted to Him, I silently and slowly say the Lord's Prayer. I pause after certain words or phrases and allow the meaning to sink in and form in my heart.

I resisted getting on my knees until last year. I didn't think physical posture was important, but I discovered it is for at least one of my prayers.

Physical posture can lead our heart and bring about a fuller experience of God. I need this physical act of humility in the morning because it sets my heart right to walk with God throughout the day.

Then, sit for a while beside the still waters of God's presence, loving and enjoying Him—grateful that He is with you. We need to learn to be with God before we do anything for God, including praying for others. When I still my mind in God's presence, my spirit is calm, and I feel loved by my heavenly Father.

Then, I pray for people and ministry. I recommend this as a great start to your day. It could last for ten minutes or an hour. This prayer acknowledges God who is over all and over your life. "In all your ways acknowledge Him and He will make straight your paths" (Proverbs 3:6, ESV). We like straight paths.

I end my day much like I began. I kneel then arise and rest in God's Presence before I rest in my bed. It makes for a deeper, more peaceful sleep.

Talk to Jesus throughout your day. It's as simple as thinking about Jesus while you go. See His smile. Smile back. Perceive Him by faith in the room you are in. Become aware of your best friend right beside you. It's a great way to do life.

Our friend Tara, an elementary school teacher, said that as she walked toward the threshold of the door at school every morning, she gave the workday to God. She asked Him to bless her kids and fill her with love for them. This is a practical, prayerful, and peaceful way to start work.

Adding conversation with God as you go through your day can replace the self-talk. We can talk to Jesus out loud, under our breath, or silently.

These conversations with God can one day become a way of life like it did for Brother Lawrence, a Carmelite monk in the 17th century. It was said of him that "his inner sense of peace was so profound that other individuals were drawn to him for spiritual direction."

His job in the monastery was kitchen work and mopping floors. At first, he despised the work. But through offering his work up to God as his gift to Him, he became a man of serene devotion.

In the 17th century book of his collected teachings, *The Practice of the Presence of God*, we read, "Brother Lawrence says of his constant conversation with God, 'I make it my business to rest in His holy presence, which I keep myself in by a habitual, silent and secret conversation with God.'"[10]

Brother Lawrence's goal was resting in God's presence with a "habitual" silent communication with Him. Knowing God like this can become a reality for all of us. Brother Lawrence was busy. He worked hard, but he made his whole life a prayer to God—an offering to Him.

It's not just for monks. Paul wrote, "Rejoice always, pray continually, give thanks in all circumstances; for this is God's will for you in Christ Jesus" (I Thessalonians 5:16–18). Through practice, we can form habits that ground our heart in the presence of God while we go throughout our day.

Continuous communion with God turns our mundane chores into purpose-filled times of devotion, silent peace, and rejoicing in God. Whether it is grocery shopping or dishwashing, all of life can become peaceful as we offer up this work to Jesus and communicate with Him as we move together to accomplish it.

---

[10] Brother Lawrence, Rewritten by Harold Chadwick, *The Practice of the Presence of God*, (Gainesville, FL: Bridge-Logos, 1999), viii.

All it takes is an internal intention to walk with God. Practice it; over time, it will become a satisfying lifestyle.

Learn the *Jesus Prayer*. I use it every day. I silently say the powerful name of Jesus as I go through my day. This simplest of prayers centers my heart in Christ more than anything while on the go.

I learned it first from the Greek Orthodox Church tradition. Their version is a one sentence prayer based in Scripture, "Lord Jesus Christ, have mercy on me, a sinner." The first phrase is taken from the Apostle Peter's profession of faith: "Simon Peter replied, 'You are the Christ, the Son of the living God'" (Matthew 16:16, ESV).

The second part is from the prayer of a tax collector and sinner: "But the tax collector stood at a distance. He would not even look up to heaven, but beat his breast and said, 'God, have mercy on me, a sinner'" (Luke 18:13).

This simple prayer takes the precious and powerful name of Jesus our Lord and pairs it with the humble confession of a sinner trusting in His mercy. I use the whole phrase sometimes: "Lord Jesus Christ, have mercy on me, a sinner." It humbles me and keeps me aware of His presence.

But most of the time, I silently and simply say "Jesus" inside my heart. Darkness flees my space, God's flame is kindled in my soul, and the river of life flows full at the mention of His name—Jesus. With practice, prayer can become as easy as breathing and renew our spiritual peace.

"No one can say, 'Jesus is Lord,' except by the Holy Spirit" (I Corinthians 12:3). The Spirit moves when our heart professes His name.

Don't worry. It's not a mantra or babbling. It's Scripture. It's God's Holy Name. And too many believers are not invoking the name of Jesus in the battle. It's a simple yet profound way to stay connected with God.

Prayer is not a production. It is a practice—a spiritual practice to keep our eyes on Jesus. You don't have to use big words or words at all to be aware of God.

During the day, calling His name in your heart can do wonders for your soul. Jesus never gets tired of hearing His name spoken within someone who desires to live in His presence. In Psalm 34:4 David wrote, "I sought the LORD, and he answered me; he delivered me from all my fears."

Worship and Music

Every night, right before we fall asleep, Dana softly sings a little verse of a hymn or praise song. It's the last thing we hear every day. I used to try to sing along with her but discovered it is best if I just listen and sing silently. It centers our hearts on Jesus. It's a sweet transition to a deep sleep.

Music has the power to transform our lives. It's God's gift to mankind to express our deepest longings and desires. Music can awaken those desires for God and open the window for a fresh breeze from heaven to revive our soul.

Music permeates heaven with sweet harmony and tranquility, and it unifies mankind in the ultimate desire—to worship God. Charles Spurgeon once taught, "God is to be praised with the voice, and the heart should go therewith in holy exultation."

Center your heart in God through praise. Sing worship songs to Jesus, and your heart will follow. Worship with music as you drive, or walk, or wait, or clean house or when you are alone.

God dwells in the praises of His people—He fills us with His Spirit, giving us the real sense of His Presence and peace. "But thou art holy, O thou that inhabitest the praises of Israel" (Psalm 22:3, KJV).

That's why Paul wrote, "Do not get drunk on wine, which leads to debauchery. Instead, be filled with the Spirit, speaking to one another with psalms, hymns, and songs from the Spirit. Sing and make music from your heart to the Lord, always giving thanks to God the Father for everything, in the name of our Lord Jesus Christ" (Ephesians 5:18–20).

Only Jesus satisfies—not partying, drunkenness, or carousing. We renounce those activities for a greater desire. Worship awakens our strongest desire for Jesus. He captivates our soul with the beauty of His holiness and the tenderness of His love. He is like nothing else. It's not even close.

Jesus had only two requirements for worship. His brief yet focused teaching is, "Yet a time is coming and has now come when the true worshipers will worship the Father in the Spirit and in truth, for they are the kind of worshipers the Father seeks. God is spirit, and his worshipers must worship in the Spirit and in truth" (John 4:23–24).

Worship is to be grounded in the truth of God's Word and come from our heart. That's it—that's what matters to the One who is receiving our worship both individually and in our gatherings.

He didn't teach about musical style or decibel levels or choirs or instruments. Those vary from age to age. But two things don't vary. It's got to be the truth. And it's got to come from the heart.

I can't carry a tune, but I do carry a playlist. Worship times in the car can center us in Jesus and release our stress. To sing and make melody in your heart, you don't have to verbalize the song. Sing along on the inside.

But sometimes, you just need to "lay your ears back and sing" as my friend Terry used to say. Turn up the volume, throw caution to the wind, and feel God's pleasure in your soul as you sing to the glory of His name. After you worship God, you will carry that tune inside you as you go about the day.

Knowing the greatness of God's nature, the weight of His glory, and the gravity of His being inspires worship and reverence. God made us for Himself. In this great relationship, our first response to knowing Him is to worship.

If *we* are the center of our thoughts, we will be miserable. Worship centers us on the Center of the Universe—Almighty God who loves us. Use music that engages your heart and draws your attention to the beautiful, the one and only love of your life, and enjoy Him forever. "I keep my eyes always on the LORD. With him at my right hand, I will not be shaken" (Psalm 16:8).

A Hard Place Into a Happy Place

Worship takes our attention off our troubles and directs our gaze upon the Lord, our safe refuge. No one can snatch us out of His hand.

Paul and Silas were in Philippi preaching the gospel, and many people were saved. Paul cast a demon out of a fortune-telling slave girl, and her masters were livid. They had used her to make a lot of money. So, they instigated a riot against Paul and Silas, who were ultimately arrested, beaten, and put in stocks in a prison.

How did they respond to this fearful and stressful situation? "About midnight Paul and Silas were praying and singing hymns to God, and the other prisoners were listening to them" (Acts 16:25).

Their bodies were in prison but their hearts were at home. They turned their eyes upon Jesus, sang His praises, and came into harmony with the music of heaven. They lived in Christ, their fortress and refuge.

That spiritual reality transcended their chains and brought victory to their soul and to others. Those prison foundations shook, and people came to know Jesus.

Circumstances will not dictate how we feel when our heart lives under the shelter of the Most High. Our security is in our dwelling place, the Lord Almighty.

Worship takes you home. And no one can take you away from there.

The greatness of our God motivated David to sing, "One thing I ask from the LORD, this only do I seek: that I may dwell in the house of the LORD all the days of my life, to gaze on the beauty of the LORD and to seek him in his temple. For in the day of trouble he will keep me safe in his dwelling; he will hide me in the shelter of his sacred tent and set me high upon a rock" (Psalm 27:4–5).

David journeyed to a tabernacle to meet with God. We journey by our spirit through the veil to meet directly with God and worship Him wherever we are. This should be our one great desire—to worship and fellowship with God, the center of our lives.

An attitude of prayer and worship keeps us abiding in the shelter and safety of God Himself. God created music for our highest purpose—to worship God. It is a sheer delight for the soul to worship the Lord.

Listen to God's Word

"So faith comes from hearing, and hearing through the word of Christ" (Romans 10:17, ESV). The Word of God speaks and reveals what is eternally true and who is eternally present with us. The Word grows our awareness of God and who He is to us.

That's why Jesus calls His teachings a rock. If we build our house on His teaching, we need not fear any weather because the house built on Jesus is eternally secure. It has substance, integrity. Everything else is sinking sand.

The world has only fleeting moments of peace because the soon-coming tides of life wash away what was built. This way of life is not sound; therefore, the house collapses. Those inside shake when the winds blow hard or when a weather forecast does not look good. They tremble because they know their foundation is weak and temporary.

The Word of God anchors us in an unshakeable Kingdom. We can have peace when the Word is abiding in us, informing us, and enlightening our understanding. If we trust in the Word and practice it, we will know peace of mind and conscience.

Apply It First to Your Heart

The truth will need to impact our hearts first, or we will become hard-hearted people who look to apply the Word to everyone but ourselves. We would then become incapable of true peace of mind.

Hypocrites moralize and complain about the world. That's how they apply the Word. They have no peace. They live in a drama as its central character and create even more drama as they judge everyone else.

I know because I've lived in hypocrisy. I created my own stress. But a person who lives by the truth applies the Word first to the drama going on inside himself to come into alignment with God. David wrote, "Behold, you delight in truth in the inward being, and you teach me wisdom in the secret heart" (Psalm 51:6, ESV).

We will be very reluctant to judge the world once the Word has judged us and transformed us by God's grace. Once inside our heart, the Word harmonizes us with the realm of God's values and God's presence.

The Word must become implanted in our soul (James 1:21) to produce godly fruit. David wrote, "I have hidden your word in my heart that I might not sin against you...I meditate on your precepts and consider your ways" (Psalm 119:11, 15).

Meditate on the Word of God to allow it to sink in and change your heart. Meditation is thoughtfully considering the Word, letting it inform your understanding and mold your inner thoughts.

For example, for a few days in my quiet time, I meditated on the crucifixion scene in which the Roman soldier pierced Jesus' side with a spear. Through reflecting on this scene, the crucifixion became personal and very real for me as the Holy Spirit caused it to come alive. My heart was moved by the gravity of Christ's suffering and the depth of His love.

Pondering the Word in our hearts helps make the historical event real to us, creating an in-depth spiritual understanding. When I read and study the Bible, I love to narrow that study down to a verse or scene that draws me in. Then I meditate on that. God speaks through His Word.

It's also great to have some Bible verses or phrases memorized. The Holy Spirit can then download them from your memory to your conscious awareness anytime and anywhere to guide and comfort, warn, and convict, or give you a word during prayer. Jesus said, "If you remain in me and my words remain in you, ask whatever you wish, and it will be done for you" (John 15:7).

When the Word of God abides in you, you can "ask for whatever you wish." How could that be? When the Word of God gets planted in you, it harmonizes you with God's will and makes prayer powerful and effective. Peace is the fruit of that harmony.

Do the Right Thing

Fidelity to the truth will cost us all we have but will give us more peace than we can ever imagine.

When Jesus stood before Pilate, we read, "'You are a king, then!' said Pilate. Jesus answered, 'You say that I am a king. In fact, the reason I was born and came into the world is to testify to the truth. Everyone on the side of truth listens to me'" (John 18:37).

Do the right thing, leave the results to God, and you will have His peace. Truth is always vindicated and proven right over time. When you are confident of that, you will be confident in your decisions and your future. Your faith in the truth has settled the matter and settled you.

We must count the cost and be willing to sacrifice all for the sake of doing what is right in the sight of God. Jesus sacrificed His life to testify to the truth. Pilate sacrificed the truth to please the people. Pilate passed, but Jesus lives.

The Word produces whatever God promises when we believe and step out. The Word is powerful, aligning us with the righteousness and action of God. The Word describes real life in all its dimensions—spiritual, relational, physical—and points the way to a life of substance and eternal purpose. This substance, purpose, and integrity are the bedrocks of peace.

Create Space

Be intentional about limiting your exposure to the fast-paced, hyped-up, attention-grabbing disordered words of the world. Practice silence. In silence, God's still small voice can be heard.

We need to disconnect from the commentary to connect with Jesus. He is the harmonizing music of the Universe—the eternal Word. It's the one necessary thing for life and peace.

Our money-driven, marketing-based culture will lure us away into worrying about "many things" if we are not disciplined. There is so much discord on social media or the news that anyone who consumes too much of it will become upset and anxious over many things.

Getting and holding our attention is the essential practice of all media. People like us are targeted by ads or news commentary programs to bolster their ratings, which translate into money. They know how to speak our language. We have to protect ourselves from their desperate reach.

I can easily get caught up by the news and fill my mind with disconcerting dramas that play out daily in the news cycle. I need to be informed but not conformed, aware but not obsessed.

So, I limit myself to no more than thirty minutes of hard news a day except when I do a news blackout for at least one week every month. That has created mental space to be captivated by Jesus.

Our world is like the story of Mary and Martha. In Luke 10:38–42, we read, "As Jesus and his disciples were on their way, he came to a village where a woman named Martha opened her home to him. She had a sister called Mary, who sat at the Lord's feet listening to what he said. But Martha was distracted by all the preparations that had to be made. She came to him and asked, 'Lord, don't you care that my sister has left me to do the work by myself? Tell her to help me!' 'Martha, Martha,' the Lord answered, 'you are worried and upset about many things, but few things are needed—or indeed only one. Mary has chosen what is better, and it will not be taken away from her.'"

While Martha was distracted and worried about many things, Mary was focused on practicing the "one thing necessary" for peace. She sat at Jesus' feet, looked into His face, and listened to His Word. She created space for intimacy.

Let's simplify our life like Mary. Jesus told Martha only a few things are needed—or indeed only one. We can be one person who slows our life down and chooses the one thing necessary.

We can train our hearts and minds with these practices to be stayed upon Jesus throughout our day. Habits help form a lifestyle of peace and joy.

I'll share one more good habit for social media viewing. It began to drain me, but I discovered a little tweak in my custom that centered my heart—I now just say a short prayer before I scroll through my feed.

I say, "God, thank You for my friends. (Pause to feel thankful.) Be with me now as I enjoy them and this time catching up." I let that sink in, and it makes all the difference for me as I scroll through my feed. Why? The purpose is love, and when we get the purpose right, God's presence and peace are experienced in the action.

When You Are Lonely

Jacob was traveling alone from Beersheba to Harran. He was leaving his family, running from Esau, and would seek a new life (and wife) far away in his mother's hometown. You can imagine how he felt.

On the journey, he stopped one night, put a stone under his head, and laid down to sleep. He had a dream in which he saw a stairway on earth, with its top extending from heaven, and angels ascending and descending on it.

Above stood the Lord, who said, "I am the Lord, the God of your father Abraham…I am with you and will watch over you wherever you go…When Jacob arose from his sleep, he thought, 'Surely the Lord is in this place, and I was not aware of it'" (Genesis 28:10–17).

We are often like Jacob and don't realize the Lord is with us—especially when we are lonely. God wants us to know He is there beside us watching over us. Think of God watching over you always—a very peaceful thought on the long journey home.

Questions for Reflection and Application

1. "Whoever dwells in the shelter of the Most High will rest in the shadow of the Almighty. I will say of the LORD, "He is my refuge and my fortress, my God, in whom I trust" (Psalm 91:1–2). Write out what this verse means to you and include a peaceful experience you have had dwelling in the shelter of the Most High. What's it like to dwell there?

2. "You keep him in perfect peace whose mind is stayed on you, because he trusts in you" (Isaiah 26:3, ESV).

    a. List three ways you can keep your mind stayed upon Jesus throughout your day.
    b. Recall an instance when you felt threatened by something during your day and you stopped to pray. How can you better develop that mindset?
    c. Tomorrow, commit to moments of silent prayer and conversation with God while you go about your day. Then reflect on what happened. Record what you learned below.

3. Describe how you worship God during a typical week.

4. How can you expand your worship of God during a typical day?

5. What podcasts, videos, or Bible Apps do you regularly use to augment your study of God's Word?

a. Are there other aids you could add into your daily routine of Bible study?

b. Practice meditating on scripture. Choose a verse or scene in the bible. Ask the Holy Spirit for help. Ponder the passage in your heart. Think about a word or phrase that speaks to you. Write down anything you felt God was saying to you through His Word.

6. Is there a particular practice mentioned in this chapter that you are inspired to try? How can you practice it today?

Chapter 9

Surrender Your Will

*"Your kingdom come, your will be done on
earth as it is in heaven."*

MATTHEW 6:10

O ur biggest fear is a key part of the cure for anxiety—
losing control. We have to lose control to give it to Jesus. That's a big step out of our comfort zone. We want to
control situations because we believe if we can exercise power
over our world, we can dispel our fear.

We think that controlling our environment can reduce
the threats to our security. At the same time, trying to control
life is the biggest source of our stress.

*Mental striving to achieve sovereignty over our lives
makes us anxious.* We will never be enough. We are not the
sovereign King over anything, including ourselves. Stress
happens when we live through our own will and understanding. This is the definition of living without God.

The first commandment is, "You shall have no other
gods before me" (Exodus 20:3). Our profession of faith is "Je-

sus is Lord" not "I'll do it my way." Jesus reigns. If we practice giving Him control, we will have peace.

Do you manage your own life? We need to quit trying to run our lives like a workplace for profit and let Jesus lead us on a journey like a Shepherd. It's stressful to be in charge of our own lives. Directing my life causes my anxieties.

Eugene Peterson addresses this idea and writes a prayer in his devotional book, *Praying with the Psalms:* "Just when I get my life arranged so that everything is under control, something happens to upset it. I need to learn, Lord, that life is not a business that I arrange and control, but a pilgrimage in which You give protection and provide guidance. Help me to learn that through Jesus Christ, my Lord. Amen."[11]

Abandon yourself to God, and you will find inner calm. Bind your will to God's will, and He will work things out according to His good pleasure.

Surrender is the posture of peace. In yielding to Jesus, we derive an assurance from trusting in our faithful Shepherd.

After Paul described our great salvation in Romans 1 through 11, he wrote about the only true and proper response to God's amazing love poured out for us: "Therefore, I urge you, brothers and sisters, in view of God's mercy, to offer your bodies as a living sacrifice, holy and pleasing to God—this is your true and proper worship" (Romans 12:1).

---

[11] Eugene Peterson, *Praying with the Psalms,* (New York, NY: Harper Collins, 1993), August 30.

A living sacrifice is alive but has given up its will to God wholly and completely—body and soul. It's the genuine response to the revelation of God's infinite mercy lavished on us sinners. Jesus took our sin and gave us His righteousness and His peace. When we surrender our lives to Jesus, this exchange happens.

Union with God

When Jesus lowered Himself to be crucified, He stepped into our shoes and bore our failings, becoming one with us in His death. "God made him who had no sin to be sin for us that in him we might become the righteousness of God" (II Corinthians 5:21).

He took my dead life and gave me His abundant life. He got my unrighteousness, and I received His righteousness. Jesus became sin, and I became a son.

We are a new creation united with Christ, and nothing can take that away. We are eternally secure in Christ. This union will never be dissolved because it depends on Jesus. And He is faithful. Our life is designed to live in union with God in Christ—walking by the Spirit, living through Christ.

We have this position in Christ as a gift. Through practice, we can also make it our experience. This gift becomes a sweet and powerful life—in union with God.

Union with God is a union of wills. Through free and willing surrender, we can live in the peace, strength, and confidence of Christ. God's will is an infinitely strong will. When we let go and live through God, we live through His willpower and His wisdom.

The Holy Spirit will carry you on the current of His power when you are yielded to Him. God wills and works through surrendered hearts. It's a joy to be one with God.

Jesus prayed for us to enjoy this close relationship even on earth: "I pray also for those who will believe in me through their message, that all of them may be one, Father, just as you are in me and I am in you. May they also be in us so that the world may believe that you have sent me" (John 17:20–21).

The pinnacle of our purpose is union with God. Nothing compares. It means our rebellion is over, and we are completely His.

In the fullness of time, we will be exalted in Christ and married to Him. This will be a blessed, eternal union that we will enjoy with Jesus. In Him, we will also be one with all the redeemed peoples who have ever lived. It's called "the communion of the saints."

We will experience unbroken harmony with God and everything and every person who is in Him. Until then, we can experience union with God through yielding to His will and His Word.

Giving God complete control will give you complete peace. It takes faith to relinquish control to God. It also takes letting go of whatever we feel in control of—finances, future, family.... Yielding our rights and our own understanding to God takes trusting in Him and His Word.

Many of us have known the joy of full surrender for seasons in our lives or maybe for a day or two. Then life happens, and we lose that sense of closeness to God.

Elisabeth Elliot said, "If my life is surrendered to God, all is well. Let me *not* grab it back, as though it were in peril in His hand but would be safer in mine!"

We "grab" our life back easily as circumstances change. To be in control is our default position. This worldly way of living is thoroughly ingrained in us and deeply grooved into our mental processes. But we can train our mind and will to be more thoroughly surrendered to God every moment of our life. It's a deeply rewarding process. Annie Hawks wrote the hymn, "I Need Thee Every Hour." The first stanza and chorus contain good reminders for us.

I need Thee every hour, most gracious Lord.
No tender voice like Thine can peace afford.
I need Thee, O, I need Thee; every hour I need Thee.
O, bless me now, my Savior, I come to Thee.

Practice Surrender

The purpose of prayer is to align our will with God's will—not God's will with ours. When I bow on my knees in the morning, I surrender all to Jesus. I let go of me and pray "Thy will be done." This starts my day in the peace of Christ.

To surrender as Jesus did to the Father, we submit our will, relinquish our rights, and yield our spirit to God. This unites us with Jesus and resurrects us in newness of life.

The rest of our day is simple. You can boil the whole duty of mankind down to this: Surrender to God's will moment by moment throughout your day and enjoy Him forever.

And here is a comforting truth written by Jean-Pierre De Caussade: "There is not a moment in which God is not present with us under the cover of some pain to be endured, some obligation or some duty to be performed, or some consolation to be enjoyed. His hand is really and truly there."[12] Abandoning yourself to God's providence in the present moment connects you with God's presence and powerful action.

When God wills something to be accomplished, He acts in the event and through it to achieve His purpose. We can experience God's peace when we are yielded to Him. He acts in even the most difficult trials with great provision, strength,

---

[12] Jean-Pierre De Caussade, Translated H. Helms, *The Joy of Full Surrender*, (Brewster MA: Paraclete Press, 1986), 33.

and assurance. We join His action through surrender and obedience.

C.S. Lewis wrote, "For the Present is the point at which time touches eternity."[13] Time touches eternity in the present. We can experience Jesus in that moment if we surrender to His will. Then we move at the impulse of His will.

That's why Jesus taught, "Therefore do not be anxious about tomorrow, for tomorrow will be anxious for itself. Sufficient for the day is its own trouble" (Matthew 6:34, ESV). Know Jesus in your now and let tomorrow worry about itself.

How Can You Know God's Will in Each Moment?

There is a time for everything. God has given us the duties of each day to fulfill according to His specific design for our lives. There is a time to drive and work, a time to play or read, a time to worship and a time to clean.

So, ask yourself, "What is the duty of the present moment? What does this time, this moment call for in me?"

Then, when you discern His will, make a transaction in your heart. Release your will, yield to God, and move with Him in what He has willed you to do for that moment. This is an inward decision—subtle but powerful.

---

[13] C.S. Lewis, *The Screwtape Letters*, (San Francisco: Harper Publishing, 2001) 75-78.

Sometimes I mark the internal switch from my will to God's will during the day with a deeper breath. Inhale, release my will, then exhale, I'm walking in His.

The goal is to live continuously surrendered to God. I'm not there yet, but this practice moves me closer. I greatly desire a more fully surrendered life because, when I walk yielded to God's will, He blesses, provides, and shows Himself in the present activity. I can see His hand in everything we do together. I'm more patient and present. It's a joy to move with God.

For example, today I am getting estimates from car repair shops to fix my mother-in-law's car. Instead of just doing this by myself, plowing ahead in my own will and understanding, I surrendered to God in it. He has willed it. It's the duty of the moment. His divine action is in the work.

The first thing I noticed was in my heart—this is a service to Judy and Wes, an act of love. This is in God's heart. That's the purpose in His will, and it became my motivation. Jesus is serving them through me. I experienced His action. We did it together.

I also noticed I wasn't rushing to get this done. God is not in a hurry. When we slow ourselves to God's pace, we move in His love and peace.

I also appreciated the people giving me an estimate. I took notice of them helping me. I thanked God for them and their work.

I had some paperwork to do when I got home. I did it in peace—a minor miracle. I'm still in the middle of helping her, and I don't feel anxious. I'm just doing the next right thing surrendered to God. It's the way of peace. He will provide.

Through surrender, God infuses His motives into our hearts, His strength to our actions, and His provision to our situations. It's a pleasure to act through God, with God, and for God. His nature becomes ours. We can become like Jesus through effective habits like this.

Integrate Your Life

We can assimilate every aspect of our life into God's will through surrender—our marriage, work, social life, etc.

A.W. Tozer wrote: "One of the great hindrances to internal peace the Christian encounters is the common habit of dividing our lives into two areas—the sacred and the secular."[14]

Compartmentalizing God, excluding Him out of our daily life, results in needless worry and stress. This mindset disconnects our will from God's, and we end up doing life on our own like a nonbeliever.

Continual surrender to God's will integrates all of our life with Him and infuses it with divine strength. This is in-

---

[14] A.W. Tozer, *The Pursuit of God,* E-book, (Abbotsford, WI: Aneko Press, 2015) 52.

tegrity. When something has integrity, it is able to stand. And for us, this strength comes from the Lord. The result is confidence.

Therefore, do everything as unto the Lord, as service to Him, a spiritual act of worship. This won't be as difficult as you think. It takes desire and surrender, not extra time. It's to be the posture of our heart.

It can become a way of life that we immensely enjoy and want. And God will help us get there. Paul wrote, "for it is God who works in you to will and to act in order to fulfill his good purpose" (Philippians 2:13).

That's a strong statement: "God works in you to will and to act." He will help us get in harmony with His motive and His movement in our life and circumstances. This will give us strength and confidence to fulfill His purposes because we know it is God at work.

We will be able to know His pleasure in all things—even the routine duties of life. They become purposeful because they are done for Him and through Him in love. We move together with God in a tandem that cannot be defeated.

So, parenting, coaching the team, dressing your child, going to the doctor, or taking a vacation will be infused with life and peace with God in control. If God has willed it, He is actively present to bless, empower, and provide.

If God's not in it, then don't do it. His Spirit and the Word will give you wisdom and discernment to know His will. Then yield to Him and act through Him.

A stanza in Fanny Crosby's hymn "Blessed Assurance" speaks of the fruit of surrender:

Perfect submission, all is at rest,
I in my Savior am happy and blest,
Watching and waiting, looking above,
Filled with His goodness, lost in His love.

Practice Acceptance

When things seem out of control, we stress out trying to figure it out. We rehearse scenarios, try to anticipate what other people may do, or try figure out how to make it through. Or we resist what God has willed by complaining about what is wrong in the world. Anxiety marks our path, and worry soaks our bed with sweat as we try to think our way out of a mess or fight through an offense.

We need to practice acceptance of what is out of our control because it is the will of God in this time or season of life. We may not understand why everything is happening, but it will give us peace of mind to know that God's got the whole situation under His control. He also has us in His hand.

We must entrust *what is* to Jesus. It doesn't mean we agree with what is going on, but until we accept it, we cannot change it. We must accept reality to gain clarity. We accept by faith.

Patience and peace birthed from this trust are virtues that will be necessary for waiting on the Lord and making wise decisions in the midst of adversity. Accepting God's will in the present gives light to the future. We can then follow His light one step at a time. He will guide us through the darkness.

God's Sovereignty

To accept God's will when it is in opposition to our own necessitates belief in two things: that God is good, and God is in control. The Bible declares these two attributes of God from Genesis to Revelation. God is our good and sovereign King.

Nothing is done or happens except that which God has foreseen from all eternity and decreed or permitted. He is sovereign over all. God never decrees evil. He never intentionally wills anything but good. But God does allow evil to exist. If He did not permit evil, then you and I would not exist.

God dignified humanity when He created us with a free will. He won't downgrade us to puppet status. We are made in His image. But with that precious and dignifying free will, He permitted the opportunity for evil, injustice, and suffering to exist through us. When we fell into sin, all of creation fell into disorder.

But God has good news—an intentional plan to redeem sinners, bring justice, vanquish evil, and cause all things to work together for "the good of those who love him, who have been called according to His purpose" (Romans 8:28).

Our will can be His will once again. God's divine order is restored and paradise is reclaimed in every surrendered heart.

It's a challenge to trust in the goodness of God when good is not apparent, and we are looking at evil, suffering, or death. But, we haven't seen the end from the beginning like God has. We must trust in God's Word in the darkness. We must lay aside our own understanding and trust in His heart.

To trust Him in dire moments is to accept those moments as willed by God. This is our act of faith. This trusting acceptance results in spiritual peace.

The Holy Spirit brings calm assurance that the situation is in God's hands, and God will be vindicated and glorified. Put it in God's hands and let yourself go to Jesus. Trust the arms that hold you and the heart that draws you close.

Joni Eareckson Tada, who was paralyzed from the shoulders down in a diving accident, wrote in her book, *The God I Love,* "Sometimes God allows what He hates to accomplish what He loves."[15]

---

[15] Joni Eareckson Tada, *The God I Love*, E-book (Grand Rapids, MI, Zondervan, 2009)

The life that Joni imagined for herself broke apart the day of her diving accident, but as she processed this life event with God over the years, she experienced the depth of God's love and peace that few of us have.

In her helplessness, God continues to make Himself known and satisfies the deep longings of her heart with His esteeming love. He empowers her to do great things for His glory through her weakness.

She goes on to write in *The God I Love*, "Sovereignty is a weighty thing to ascribe to the nature and character of God. Yet if He were not sovereign, He would not be God. The Bible is clear that God is in control of everything that happens."[16]

As our faith in God's sovereignty grows, our experience of God's peace deepens. No one can explain the full reason why everything happens. We won't understand it all until we get to heaven. But on earth we can come to harmony with God through acceptance. Then, we can live in the wisdom of faith.

Our Model for Acceptance

In the Garden of Gethsemane, Jesus showed us the gospel way of prayer when the day of evil or suffering arrives: "Then he said to them, 'My soul is overwhelmed with sorrow to the point of death. Stay here and keep watch with me.' Going a

---

[16] Joni Eareckson Tada, *The God I Love*, E-book (Grand Rapids, MI, Zondervan, 2009)

little farther, he fell with his face to the ground and prayed, 'My Father, if it is possible, may this cup be taken from me. Yet not as I will, but as you will'" (Matthew 26:38–39).

Jesus wrestled with the will of God with deep emotion and brokenness in prayer. Like Him, our soul can be overwhelmed with anxiety, stress, or sorrow over God's decreed or permissive will in our circumstances.

Jesus questioned God to see if it was possible not to have to drink that cup of suffering. He wrestled with this because He had to know if the cup was willed by God because it was filled with injustice, evil, punishment, and God's wrath.

After praying for the third time, Jesus knew God willed for Him to drink from that cup. Jesus then yielded to the will of the Father in the day of evil. This acceptance ended His emotional anguish and acute stress. The inner struggle was over.

Acceptance of God's will removes mental anguish and stress. We no longer fight it, stress over it, complain, or put up mental resistance once we accept it as the will of God. We quit striving to find our way around it. A lot of mental suffering is associated with not accepting what is God's will.

Jesus showed us how to grapple with the issue in prayer. He prayed for the cup to be removed if possible—more than once. He wrestled until He knew.

Then He surrendered to God's sovereign will. Afterwards, Jesus obeyed God with courage and strength one step at a time. He moved forward with conviction and faced the most intense suffering ever known.

All of us are called to walk in the footsteps of Jesus through our Gethsemanes and our dying moments. Call out to God. Wrestle with the injustice of it. Ask if it is possible for the cup to pass. You must grapple with it to know for sure because you will be pressed beyond your own strength.

You have to know. Then, if it is God's will, let go and submit to Him. Trust Him. Accept it, and He will lead you through it like He did for Jesus, giving you His strength and assurance.

In His trial, Jesus was slow to speak, did not repay evil for evil, but overcame evil with good. That evil day became resurrection, vindication, redemption, and glory to God's holy name.

You can be assured that God will work through your pain, acceptance, and obedience for the glory of His holy name and your eternal good.

The Thorn in Your Side

Paul took this gospel template from the life of Jesus and applied it when his thorn in the flesh was given. Paul wrote, "because of these surpassingly great revelations. Therefore, in order to keep me from becoming conceited, I was given a thorn in my flesh, a messenger of Satan, to torment me. Three times I pleaded with the Lord to take it away from me" (II Corinthians 12:7–8).

He describes his thorn as "a messenger of Satan." It was the day of evil for him. He was in much anguish like Jesus. And like Jesus, Paul prayed three times as he wrestled with God, asking Him to take away the thorn.

Then God replied, "My grace is sufficient for you, for my power is made perfect in weakness." At this, Paul accepted the thorn as willed by God. Then the joy and peace of Jesus returned to His soul.

God's power was made perfect in Paul's weakness. He wrote: "Therefore I will boast all the more gladly about my weaknesses, so that Christ's power may rest on me. That is why, for Christ's sake, I delight in weaknesses, in insults, in hardships, in persecutions, in difficulties. For when I am weak, then I am strong" (II Corinthians 12:9–10).

Like Jesus, he was able to get there because he wrestled until he knew that his weakness was God's will, even though the messenger was evil. He accepted the thorn in faith and experienced divine strength and peace. We can have this peace if we take this way.

No one wants these thorns, these messengers of Satan who weaken us. They are evil. But God has willed it for a greater, more important purpose. This reminds us of another important testimony of the power of acceptance.

Bloom Where You Are Planted

Out of envy, Joseph's brothers sold him to slave traders who took him to Egypt. I'm sure Joseph was anxious and afraid on much of that journey. But somewhere along the way, his faith in God as sovereign King took hold. He accepted his lot and bloomed where he was planted by the will of God.

He did not complain. He did not fight. He did not disobey God. He cleared his heart of any hint of bitterness and resentment. He commended himself to the dominion of God and moved forward in peace. God opened doors, then He closed them. Joseph accepted this and followed.

Joseph was faithful in the little things. He lived one day at a time. Integrity formed in him. God had a plan...a plan for God's glory and Joseph's highest good. That plan necessitated faith and character.

When Joseph's brothers turned to Egypt for food during famine, Joseph eventually revealed himself to his brothers. They were very afraid because his brothers knew they had sinned grievously against him.

But Joseph's response surprised them: "His brothers then came and threw themselves down before him. 'We are your slaves,' they said.

But Joseph said to them, 'Don't be afraid. Am I in the place of God? You intended to harm me, but God intended it for good to accomplish what is now being done, the saving of many lives. So then, don't be afraid. I will provide for you and your children.' And he reassured them and spoke kindly to them" (Genesis 50:18–21).

Joseph made peace with his brothers because he had made peace with God. He had developed a tremendous faith in God's sovereignty as evidenced by his reply to his brothers, "Am I in the place of God?" Joseph was declaring that God has power and dominion over all things.

When we try to take God's place as sovereign, anxiety and stress will mark our days. Joseph believed God in the dark valleys, accepted His will, and trusted His plan. Joseph overcame evil with good.

Joseph told his fearful brothers, "You intended to harm me, but God intended it for good to accomplish what is now being done, the saving of many lives."

Your highest purpose will be birthed from your greatest pain when it is accepted by faith and lived out in devotion to God. God's power will manifest in your weakness and move you forward in His plan.

Be faithful in the small things. Bloom where you are planted. Love your people. Many will be saved.

Francois Fenelon wrote: "No more restless uncertainties, no more anxious desires, no more impatience at the place we are in; for it is God who has placed us there, and who holds us in his arms. Can we be unsafe where he has placed us?"[17]

---

[17] Francois Fenelon, AZQuotes.com, (Wind and Fly LTD, 2022), https://www.azquotes.com

We cannot be unsafe where God has placed us. God has ordained our days from the beginning. He speaks to us in all things, especially in our suffering and anxieties. He has a word for us in all circumstances.

Let's accept what God has willed. He will give us courage for the journey and assurance that the journey will be good and for God's eternal glory.

A Pattern for the Promises

Job and his wife were perfect contrasts—one could not accept what had happened, and one did. Job and his wife lost their family and all their possessions. Then Job lost his health.

We read their responses: "His wife said to him, 'Are you still maintaining your integrity? Curse God and die!' He replied, 'You are talking like a foolish woman. Shall we accept good from God, and not trouble?' In all this, Job did not sin in what he said" (Job 2:9–10).

Job's wife resisted and fought. Job trusted and accepted. Accepting trouble as the will of God will give you the patience of Job as you persevere in your trial. This is fertile ground for God's faithfulness to be shown to you.

This patience and perseverance will see you through to the promises. In the end, God blessed Job with comfort, friends, family, flocks, and herds.

Accept everything God sends, whether its blessing or adversity. Your cross won't last forever, but your faithfulness in accepting it will glorify God's name forever.

A Test of Acceptance

As I worked in my office, our church secretary buzzed my phone and told me that my cousin Lucy wanted to speak with me. I was excited to talk to her. I picked up the phone and said, "Hello, Lucy!" She replied, "Jake, Jenny (my sister) died this morning in a car wreck."

Immediately, I knew I had two choices. Turn away from God in anger and grieve on my own or cry out to God who had just taken my sister.

I fell to my knees, broke in a million pieces, cried out to Jesus, and sobbed. I heaved with grief at His feet, knowing all along that He could have saved her. That hurt me too. But, I cast myself at the feet of Him who holds our hope. I went with Jesus—all in.

Job said, "Though He slay me, I will hope in Him. Nevertheless I will argue my ways before Him" (Job 13:15, NASB).

That is a healthy way to be when you are knocked off your feet. Argue or wrestle, question or cry, but struggle with God in prayer with a purpose—to come to the knowledge and acceptance of His will.

Take the time, but don't just sit on it. Process it to eventual acceptance. Jesus, the Pioneer of our faith, blazed a trail through this wilderness of hurt for us to follow. He is our model for peace.

1. Pray and be honest with God. Pray again. And again.

2. Know God's will.
3. Accept God's will.
4. Obey God in peace and His will be done.

There is no "I" or "me" in this template. It's Jesus-centered and God glorifying. That's how to overcome our anxiety in a very troubling situation.

A Prayer of Serenity

American theologian Reinhold Niebuhr wrote a prayer commonly referred to as the "Serenity Prayer" that has helped many people find peace during perplexing adversity:

"God, grant me the serenity to accept the things I cannot change, courage to change the things I can, and wisdom to know the difference."[18]

Serenity comes through acceptance of what is not in our control. Whether its traffic on a busy freeway, what other people think of us, or aging, we are to accept "what is," surrender to Jesus in it, then do His will.

With His strength and provision, we can walk through our darkest valley one step at a time without fear. God your Good Shepherd will take care of you and lead you through to higher ground.

---

[18] Kaplan, Justin, ed. (2002), Reinhold Niebuhr (1892–1971), *Bartlett's Familiar Quotations (17th ed.)*, (Boston, MA: Little Brown and Company, 1943), 735.

Questions for Reflection and Application

1. Abandon yourself to God and you will find inner calm. Bind your will to God's will, and He will work things out according to His good pleasure. Surrender is the posture of peace. What are the elements involved in a personal decision to surrender to God?

    a. Pause now. Take a moment to surrender your will to God before considering the following question.
    b. How could you form a habit to surrender to God during your day?

2. Why did Jesus pray three times, "My Father, if it be possible, let this cup pass from me; nevertheless, not as I will, but as you will" (Matthew 26:39)?

3. Describe a time when you wrestled with God's will in prayer. Why is that important to get to acceptance?

4. Job accepted trouble as the will of God. "His wife said to him, 'Are you still maintaining your integrity? Curse God and die!' He replied, 'You are talking like a foolish woman. Shall we accept good from God, and not trouble?' In all this, Job did not sin in what he said" (Job 2:9–10).

a. What was the difference between Job's acceptance and his wife's non-acceptance?

b. List reasons why we have trouble getting to acceptance of God's will.

c. Is there a circumstance that you have not accepted yet as a part of God's will for this season of your life? If so, describe your hesitancy.

5. Consider entrusting a source of your anxiety to Jesus and His sovereign will. Talk to God about giving Him control of it. Record your prayer experience.

Chapter 10

Ground Your Soul

*"Be completely humble and gentle; be patient, bearing
with one another in love."*

EPHESIANS 4:2

T he most important virtue in the kingdom of God is
humility. It is the gate through which we acquire the
greatest virtues—love, righteousness, hope, peace....

When someone visits the Church of the Nativity in Beth-
lehem, they must enter through a door that is 4'3" high. Most
every adult bows to enter.

Then they make their way to the grotto or cave where it
is believed Jesus was born. After his birth, his little body was
laid in a manger and gazed upon by animals and lowly shep-
herds. God chose these humble beginnings for a reason.

Andrew Murray wrote, "Humility, the place of entire
dependence on God, is the first duty and the highest virtue of
the creature, and the root of every virtue. And so pride, or the
loss of this humility, is the root of every sin and evil."[19]

---

[19] Andrew Murray, *Humility: The Journey Toward Holiness,* (Bloomington, MN:
Bethany House, 2002), 16.

Pride was our downfall in the Garden of Eden. Pride is the biggest enemy of humanity today. It is the mountain inside us that must be removed to be in harmony with God, for "God opposes the proud…" (James 4:6).

It's not just that God doesn't help the proud. He opposes them. Pride must go for peace to come.

The Desert

The Bible tells us, "Now Moses was a very humble man, more humble than anyone else on the face of the earth" (Numbers 12:3). That's why he was called a friend of God. He wasn't perfect, but he had this virtue of meekness that opened doors for him with God.

The meekness of Moses was formed through humiliation and humble work. He fled Pharaoh in fear and failure. He eventually accepted his new normal in the Midian desert as a shepherd. He was faithful in that small work for forty years.

This time of formation in the desert was the most important season for Moses. It will be for us too. The desert purges us and prepares us.

Moses let go of the Egyptian way in the desert. He accepted his place in the desert and did what God had ordained him to do—tend sheep.

The New Testament definition of *humility* comes from the Greek word *tapeinoo,* which literally means *making oneself low or close to the ground.* The Latin root of the word humble, humus, means *the ground or the earth.* If we ground ourselves in genuine humility, then we ground ourselves in God.

The desert experience helped Moses stay grounded and dependent on God. After forty years in the desert, he didn't trust in himself or the Egyptian way anymore. He had been humbled and his life had been simplified. That's the fertile ground God uses.

Then God spoke out of a burning bush and called Moses to lead His people out of bondage—all two and a half million of them. This time, Moses would do it God's way—in concert with Him.

Pride was our downfall, but grace has been our uplifting. When we stay grounded in humility, we will stay uplifted in grace.

God's Own Humble Heart

Today, the most humble person who has ever lived is Jesus. He teaches us, "Come to me, all you who are weary and burdened, and I will give you rest. Take my yoke upon you and learn from me, for I am gentle and humble in heart, and you will find rest for your souls. For my yoke is easy and my burden is light" (Matthew 11:28–30).

The heart of Jesus is gentle and humble. He is not angry with us but is patient and kind. His voice is gentle and true.

He does not withhold His fellowship when we have a bad day.

He invites the weary and burdened to come to Him. He gives us rest. Humility is personified in the heart of Jesus. Through fellowship with Jesus, we are unburdened and our mind put at ease.

Communion with Jesus takes place heart to heart—humble, dependent heart to humble, divine heart. This creates a close bond of intimacy like a small child has with a parent.

When we fellowship with Jesus like this, we don't have a worry in the world. Our burden is light. We rest. Our stress is relieved. His sheer presence casts out fear.

We will experience Jesus down low where His heart is—He is humble. He won't pull us down there. We must freely choose to go there, to humble ourselves. Humility is a free will lowering of ourselves for the sake of Christ.

To know Him and become like Him is our highest call. Humility is a crucial element in that narrow road that leads to life.

Paul wrote, "I want to know Christ—yes, to know the power of his resurrection and participation in his sufferings, becoming like him in his death" (Philippians 3:10).

Knowing Jesus heart to heart necessitates a participation in His sufferings. Pride manifests itself in independence and self-assertion—two key components of the philosophy of our culture. When Jesus taught that if anyone wished to follow Him "let them take up their cross," it would mean that hu-

miliation and submission to God would be part of their journey just like His.

But it has the divine purpose to form Christ in us. So, we
"must follow in His footsteps" (I Peter 2:21) and "walk as Jesus walked" (I John 2:6). But remember that crucifixion
brings resurrection into your new, exalted nature. Each willing act of obedience causes our pride to die a little more and
loosen its grip on us.

Humility Redeems Your Worth

Lowering oneself is not to be confused with Satan's accusa-
tion that you are worthless—that's absolutely a lie. The blood
of Jesus Christ declares your infinite worth. The price God
paid to redeem you and make you His child is beyond compare. The Father and the Son paid an infinite price for you.
That's who you are to Him—dearly loved.

Humility sheds the false promise of self-esteem for the
sure promise of God's infinite esteem. That's the esteem we
are destined to know by grace.

In all our painful trials, Jesus calls us to come to Him—
and His gentle and humble heart will lift us. Then your humiliation will be vanquished, and you will be left with a
humble heart that has been exalted by God.

Jesus didn't remain on the cross. Our suffering in obedience is temporary. After pride suffers another death, the
dignifying lift of God's Spirit in your humble obedience will

come and carry you through until your obedience is complete.

God will move you forward in a "love that surpasses knowledge" (Ephesians 3:19) and a "peace that transcends all understanding" (Philippians 4:7). Obedience will become your resurrection to new life.

Meekness Matters

A meek heart communes with God and finds rest for the soul. Entering His rest renews our spirit. God's gentle heart heals our wounded heart and makes us whole. His kind heart embraces us and holds us close.

A.W. Tozer wrote, "Jesus calls us to His rest, and meekness is His method. The meek man cares not at all who is greater than he, for he has long ago decided that the esteem of the world is not worth the effort."[20]

We must take Tozer's view of the world's esteem in order to "lower ourselves." If we realize that the esteem of the world is not worth the effort and stress to gain it, then we will be on our way to humility—the humility of Christ. We must believe in the humble way of Jesus. Jesus taught us, "Blessed are the meek, for they will inherit the earth" (Matthew 5:5).

The meek forget about themselves and enjoy God in everything and everybody. Prideful people can only try to enjoy

---

[20] A.W. Tozer, *The Pursuit of God* E-book, (Abottsford, WI: Aneko Press, 2015), 49.

themselves—an empty cup. Their lofty image has to be kept up, tended to, and defended at all costs. It's wearisome and distressing. They are afraid of meekness.

Meekness carries strength and courage in a kind and gentle package. That's the nature of Christ. We need not be afraid of being meek when rightly understood.

A W. Tozer went on to write, "The meek man is not a human mouse afflicted with a sense of his own inferiority. Rather he may be in his moral life as bold as a lion and as strong as Samson; but he has stopped being fooled about himself. He has accepted God's estimate of his own life. He knows he is as weak and helpless as God has declared him to be, but paradoxically, he knows at the same time that he is in the sight of God of more importance than angels. In himself, nothing; in God, everything. That is his motto."[21]

That last phrase, "In himself, nothing; in God, everything" is the paradox of humility. Humility, our nothingness, is the key that opens the door to everything, our new godly nature.

We embrace humility, and God's character forms in us—a gentle strength, a kind yet firm resolve, a righteous but non-judgmental spirit. This pure, peaceful, and courageous nature is who you really are—a son or daughter of God.

---

[21] A.W. Tozer, *The Pursuit of God* E-book, (Abottsford, WI: Aneko Press, 2015), 50.

The Nature of Humility

Humility is a proper view of oneself. We don't get this proper view by comparing ourselves to others. That's a formula for misery. As a young ambitious minister, I used to compare myself with other ministers. I soon discovered it's self-defeating.

That worldly standard will always impart to us the lie "I'm not enough." That lie is hard to live under. Most of us have it ingrained in us through our perception of how things work in this fallen world. But that is not the standard God uses.

We need to rid ourselves of Satan's accusations. In Christ, there is *no* condemnation. From the gospel, we learn the truth of our fallen condition and God's loving remedy at the same time—the death, burial, and resurrection of Jesus. Those twin truths simultaneously humble us and lift us.

We sinners are forevermore God's children by grace. This is an unchangeable truth that God has already declared over those who believe. That's why humility doesn't self-denigrate.

God's standard for His children has always been His glory, His likeness. That's why Jesus taught, "Be perfect, therefore, as your heavenly Father is perfect" (Matthew 5:48). That's the highest, most exalted calling in the world. Nothing comes close. We all fall short of His glory.

God will not lower His standards, thereby reducing our worth. But He will raise lowly sinners up to those lofty heights by His grace. We experience God's elevating grace through humility and trust.

This is the supreme exaltation, the most awesome dignity of mankind—to share in the glory of Jesus Christ, God's Son. But just knowing about our position in Christ isn't enough.

When we know something through a merely intellectual understanding, our mind says, "So what! What difference does that make?" Then it returns to what it knows by experience—which could have even been a bad experience.

Knowing—real knowing that makes a difference—is through a personal encounter with the life-changing truth. When we experience Jesus in our acts of humility and love, our mind says, "Now I *really* know! I know the humble and gentle heart of Jesus and the power of His resurrection." Then our mind is all in for whatever it takes to humble ourselves.

The Tough News about Humility

One thing we have to accept before we practice humility— our pride has to go. It doesn't go easily.

Pride promotes itself, defends itself, and justifies itself. It only views situations through self-interest—even Bible verses. It judges others, complains about leaders, offends easily, demands its way, and asserts its will. We must first count the cost of losing our pride before we can acquire humility.

Your ego will be wounded. Your pride will be hurt. You will feel some humiliation. All of this is to happen as a willing act in the tests of obedience that requires meekness. We must trust this is the way—the way of Jesus—because our pride dies hard.

Remember resurrection is bonded to each cross we willingly take up to be faithful to Jesus. Freedom over anxiety will track with the formation of this genuine humility.

Practices to Form Humility—Follow the Example of Jesus

Paul describes the ultimate humility of Christ and exhorts us to follow His example: "Do nothing out of selfish ambition or vain conceit. Rather, in humility value others above yourselves, not looking to your own interests but each of you to the interests of the others. In your relationships with one another, have the same mindset as Christ Jesus: "Who, being in very nature God, did not consider equality with God something to be used to his own advantage; rather, he made himself nothing by taking the very nature of a servant, being made in human likeness. And being found in appearance as a man, he humbled himself by becoming obedient to death—even death on a cross! Therefore God exalted him to the highest place and gave him the name that is above every name" (Philippians 2:3–9).

Let's consider four gospel commands listed in the above passage that will ground our soul in the humility of Christ and lift it to the heights with God.

1. Adopt the Attitude of Christ

What should be our mindset toward other people? In verse 3, we read that humility "values others above oneself." It was the attitude of Jesus.

Developing Christ-like humility results in real friends who love each other. It's hard to unlearn our "me-focused" popular mindset and to adopt the attitude of esteeming others above ourselves. But this attitude bears good fruit.

In his book *The Purpose Driven Life,* Rick Warren wrote, "Humility is not thinking less of yourself, but thinking of yourself less. Humility is thinking more of others."[22]

Consider the people you like to be around. What are they like? What characteristics do they have? It's probably the person who thinks highly of you and wants to know how you are doing. They are interested in what's going on in your life. They ask you questions, and then do something our society lacks—they listen.

They don't listen to respond or to judge. They listen to know you. It's genuine. They care. They put you first in the conversation. That's a Christ-like attitude.

---

[22] Rick Warren, *The Purpose Driven Life,* (Grand Rapids, MI: Zondervan, 2002), 148.

James wrote: "My dear brothers and sisters, take note of this: Everyone should be quick to listen, slow to speak and slow to become angry" (James 1:19).

Your humble friends take the initiative in the conversation by listening and asking you about your life. They want to "catch up" with you because they are interested in you and your family. The meek have character and make good friends. They have a peaceful life in Christ.

We can't be the main character in the scenes of our lives and be humble or happy. In the meek, self-importance has been replaced by love that focuses on others first—not because they have to, but because Christ has been formed in them.

Practice listening to people without thinking about how you are going to respond to what they say. It's not about you in this moment. It's about them. Give them the gift of yourself. It's a golden gift from a golden rule.

My friend Rocky and his parents informally adopted me into their family after my dad died. Among the many things they did, the one that stands out the most was that they listened to me. In our visits and on our vacations, they asked questions about my life. They cared about me.

To this day, they rejoice with me in my journey to God and sympathize with me in my hardships. They forget themselves and focus on me for long stretches in our conversations. This has bonded me with them over the years. They are like family to me.

If your friends aren't seeking to know you, that's no problem. Jesus cares for you. He listens. It takes humility to become a good listener.

Good listeners will always have friends. Their friends will reciprocate in due time or others will. Until then, just take pleasure in knowing your friends. This practice will form the attitude of Christ who esteemed us over Himself.

We can value others highly because God has valued us. When we receive dignifying love in our humble condition, then we can give dignifying love to others with a humble heart. We reflect what is in us to the world.

Jesus was thinking about us on the cross. He put us first. God chose to consider us of infinite value and sent His only Son to redeem us. That's humility and dignifying love—the mindset of Christ.

2. Take the Nature of a Servant

Our Philippians passage stated that Jesus took "the nature of a servant, being made in human likeness." That's the model for every human being as God restores His image in us—to become a servant.

Christians get filled up with God's pleasure when they pour themselves out in God's service to people. Serving blesses everyone, but especially the one serving people. We experience God acting with us when we serve.

Taking a meal to a neighbor, helping a widow with a home repair, visiting a friend in the hospital, doing the unpleasant task at work...This union of attitude and action is purposeful and peaceful. Service gets the focus off of us and onto God's mission.

Servant leadership starts in the home and should permeate our participation in church life, employment, citizenship...This type of leadership promotes peace because leaders forget about themselves to empower the people around them. They come alongside people and enable them to discover their mission and equip them to serve. It's all about helping others to shine and succeed.

Servants also do the little things that are necessary but unnoticed. God sees what we do in secret and will reward us. This secret service produces character. Someone said, "Character is what you do when no one is watching." This peaceful way of life frees us from the need to be noticed by men to win their approval. For believers, we are serving God as we serve people. He sees, and He rewards.

3. Gospel Obedience

In our Philippians passage we read, "He humbled himself by becoming obedient to death—even death on a cross!" We will have many opportunities to humble ourselves to obey Christ.

Humility will be formed through these times of obedience—turning the other cheek, going the extra mile, sharing a gospel witness...We will become more humble like Jesus and experience the peace and joy of Christ's resurrected nature.

For example, when we offend our brother, we are to go to them and offer them a sincere apology. This is a humbling thing to do. It's also the right thing to do.

In the process, our ego will loosen its grip on us, and we will become more like Jesus. It's peace-making both for the relationship and the person apologizing.

Saying "I am sorry" and feeling sorrowful is the gospel being lived out. It's acknowledging our shortcomings, going to the person we have offended, and apologizing. Coworkers and family members will appreciate you for it.

4. Identify with the Weak

Paul also directs believers to "Live in harmony with one another. Do not be proud, but be willing to associate with people of low position. Do not be conceited" (Romans 12:16).

The exhortation to be willing "to associate with people of low position" is sandwiched between "Do not be proud" and "Do not be conceited." This is a pride-busting, ego-deflating, Jesus-loving commandment that is meant to form the humility of Christ in us.

Jesus associates Himself with lowly, frail, needy humans like us. Jesus stands with those who are the least-esteemed people in the world and calls us to stand by His side, their side.

During my mission in Africa, I would come home on most nights pretty spent after working as a basketball coach and student leader at the University of Zambia. I wanted some "me time." I wanted to socialize with peers.

But, I started noticing the yard worker and gate keeper, Ojohn and Justin Mwape, cousins who lived in a crude dwelling on our premises. They were poor and uneducated.

They could speak only broken English. I didn't want to spend my off time with them. They couldn't help me recharge. They would be needy. I would be the giver.

But I knew God was calling me to them. I finally surrendered to His will and began spending evenings with them.

We would sit by the fire and talk. They told me stories of their experiences with crocodiles, snakes, and buffalo. I shared with them stories of American life.

They were from the bush, meaning in the middle of nowhere in Africa. They had come to the capital city seeking to make some money for their families. They recently got their jobs with the Baptist Mission opening our gate and keeping our grounds. I started to look forward to our times together.

I discovered they were animists, worshiped their ancestors, and had some Christian influence that wasn't orthodox. I shared Jesus with them. They gave their lives to Him. They were all in.

I gave them two Bibles and some material in their own language from our mission. Then, every night around their campfire became a meeting for discipleship and fellowship. We had a great time in the Lord. We got to know each other very well.

After a year or so, they told me they wanted to go back to their village in the bush to share Jesus and start a church. I was shocked. They were giving up a prized job making decent money, but they wanted to go lead their people to Jesus. I sensed the Lord calling them, so I wanted to help.

With a donation from a friend in the church where I grew up, I bought a hundred Bibles in their tribal language. They wrote home and told their family we would be coming on a certain date.

Early one morning after basketball season, all three of us loaded up in the Baptist Volkswagen van and made the long journey into the African bush.

It was about 4:00 p.m. when we literally reached the end of the road. I could see a crowd forming as we eased to a stop—and it kept getting larger. The whole village knew we were coming on that day. They were coming out to greet us. I unbuckled to get out, but my friends told me to stay in the van. People were coming with machetes—but they looked happy.

Then the men began cutting small trees and bushes, removing rocks, and calling me to inch forward. All the while, they were laughing, working, and rejoicing. I will never forget inching forward in that van as a road was being built just ahead of me. No vehicle had ever been to their village. An hour later, we were there.

I had a true African Jesus experience that week. I slept in a hut on a stick bed, ate warthog, and hunted at night with a slingshot and a flashlight. I visited with their African chief who invited me to return and hunt elephants with him.

When Sunday rolled around, almost everyone in the surrounding villages came to our first outdoor church service. Many souls were saved.

I left a few days later, thanking God for my association with Ojohn and Justin Mwape, our gate keeper and yard worker at the mission. I never returned to their village, but the imprint of Christ through my fellowship with them has been permanently etched in my soul.

Our associations with "the weak" can be life-changing because Jesus is present in them. They resemble Jesus in His passion.

Isaiah writes of our Messiah: "He had no beauty or majesty to attract us to him, nothing in his appearance that we should desire him. He was despised and rejected by mankind, a man of suffering, and familiar with pain. Like one from whom people hide their faces he was despised, and we held him in low esteem" (Isaiah 53:2–4).

The lowly are like Jesus to us. He stands with them calling us to Himself. Humanity held Jesus in low esteem on earth. That is the sad truth. Why? He was a man of suffering. People who are in pain and captivity are not esteemed by this world.

But Jesus stepped into our shoes and suffered willingly before the people of the world. He was humiliated before them. It looked like they won and He lost. But he was overcoming them by giving His life in love. Jesus took their fists to His face and insults to His character without retaliation.

No one in their flesh wants to be associated with someone like that. Even the followers of Jesus left His side and did not associate with Him when He was bound and taken away. It's not natural to come alongside someone who has lost their position, power, and esteem of others or never had it.

We can humble ourselves and find Jesus in the "least of these my brethren." We are not to play rescuer. There is only one who can do that. Don't take that burden on yourself for the whole world.

Just be sensitive to the Spirit who will reveal to you the ones for you to come alongside and befriend. In identifying with the lowly, we will get over ourselves and humility will form.

Humility of heart bonds us with Jesus transforming our lowly nature into His divine likeness. These practices will hurt our ego but heal our soul.

Questions for Reflection and Application

1. "For those who exalt themselves will be humbled, and those who humble themselves will be exalted" (Matthew 23:12).

    a. What does this verse mean to you?

    b. List some of the practical benefits of living with humility.

    c. A.W. Tozer wrote, "In himself nothing, in God everything." What steps could you take to make this more of a reality for you?

2. Many people mistake *meekness* for *weakness*. Reflect on this quote, "Meekness carries strength and courage in a kind and gentle package." What does that quote mean to you?

    a. Think about a person you know who exhibits meekness. Describe the attributes of meekness as you think about them.

    b. What other attributes do you see in them that result from their Christ-like meekness?

3. Reflect on a way you have humbled yourself. How did you grow through it?

    a. How good are you at apologizing? Is there someone you should apologize to today? Write what you would say.

    b. How could you become a better listener?

4. Recall a time when your pride was hurt.

   a. How did you respond?

   b. How can you respond differently the next time so that the humility of Christ forms in you through the experience?

5. Who has God brought into your life that might be "one of the least of these His brethren"? How can you best love and serve them?

Chapter 11

Accept Yourself

"The second is this: 'Love your neighbor as yourself.'"

MARK 12:31

We can't be at peace with God and not try to make peace within ourselves and with our neighbor. Ken Sande in his classic book *The Peacemaker* wrote, "There are three dimensions to the peace that God offers to us through Christ: peace with God, peace with one another, and peace within ourselves."[23]

Our final two practices will focus on having peace within ourselves and peace with our fellow man. We can love our neighbor *as* ourselves only when we have a healthy love *for* ourselves. This love for self is not a narcissistic, self-absorbed love, but rather a tender Spirit-inspired acceptance of our humble self in Christ.

To share God's view of you, you must see yourself in grace and realize how precious you are. Then, that view will be reflected to others in kindness and esteem. Knowing and

---

[23] Ken Sande, *The Peacemaker* E-book edition, (Grand Rapids, MI: Baker Books, 2012), 607.

experiencing your new identity in Christ will bring love for your neighbor and peace within yourself.

Our relationship with God travels down the same road in our heart as our relationship with ourself and others. That's one reason why the two greatest commandments are alike—loving God and loving our neighbor *as ourselves*. Everything in the Word of God flows through these two commands—including peace.

We need to accept ourselves as we are—unconditionally and completely—the way God does. A lot of anxiety stems from trying to be good enough. That's a never-ending cycle of failure. There is no peace in working for self-acceptance.

We cannot change unless we first accept ourselves just as we are in God's grace. Otherwise, striving to be good enough and self-condemnation will fill our lives with stress.

The fact is that sin separated us from God, ourself, and our neighbors. We died when we sinned in the garden because we lost our likeness to and connection with God. It's been a frantic search ever since to restore ourselves with no success.

We are estranged from God, ourselves, and others, and no work of our own can restore us. We need to accept God's grace for ourselves. Then, and only then, will we have love for the world and peace within.

Why Is It Hard to Accept Ourselves?

It's difficult to accept ourselves when we don't know who we are in Christ. We look to religion, our world, others, or ourselves to define us. We adopt our own expectations, our own standard of success, or even God's law to define us. We have an image of who we prefer to be.

We fall short of these adopted standards and are oppressed by our shortcomings. That's why at the core of the human condition is pride and self-hatred. The law condemns us. The world rejects us. Our thoughts oppress us. Every adopted standard denigrates us—except one.

Jesus is the good news that rescues us, accepts us, and restores our worth. You will never, ever fall short of God's grace in Christ. He has saved you from all your sin—past, present, and future.

You will never lack in grace once you are in grace. You can be at peace in Christ. We really are saved from anxiety by grace.

The world we grow up in bombards us with images to identify with and strive toward. We internalize our environment. We gravitate toward a social identity group and assimilate their cultural design for happiness. It gets ingrained in us. Teenagers have to "find out who they are" and begin identifying with a group they "fit in with."

Instead of knowing who we are in Christ, we try to find who we are in the world. We buy into self-determination or get sucked into someone's game of life. It's oppressive. Self-definition puts us in disharmony with our Creator.

You were meant first and foremost to be loved by God and find your restored identity in His image. Who you really are is not conferred by the law but imparted to you by God Himself. It's a gift.

How Do I Find My True Identity?

We have learned important truth from God's Word in previous chapters about who we are in Christ. God will also communicate our new identity through quietness and trust.

We are to simply "be still and know that I am God" (Psalm 46:10). Knowing God in stillness and trust is the way to know ourselves and our new nature. God reflects His likeness to those who have been remade in it.

When King David was afraid, he wrote, "My heart says of you, 'Seek his face!' Your face, Lord, I will seek" (Psalm 27:8). If we really want to know someone, we must look into their face.

We won't be able to literally see God with our eyes until we meet Him in heaven, but we can perceive God's favor toward us through faith. We need to see that—God's favor. It's our salvation in every way—even from anxiety.

John Newton wrote a line in the hymn "Amazing Grace" that says, "I once was lost but now I am found; was blind but now I see." Now I see! What did He see? He saw the light of God's grace, God's esteeming love. He saw God's smile.

John Newton, the guilt-plagued and hopeless slave trader, was found by God's grace and given a precious gift—His eternal favor. Experience that grace, and we will know who we are. Grace is God's favor toward an undeserving sinner.

God's face shines on every believer. His face is glorious and gracious. He shines on you. Through child-like trust and humility, you can draw your identity from God's image being reflected to you.

Paul wrote, "For God, who said, 'Let light shine out of darkness,' made his light shine in our hearts to give us the light of the knowledge of God's glory displayed in the face of Christ" (II Corinthians 4:6).

We can perceive God's favor toward us in a direct personal relationship with Him. The closer we get, the more we grow in our perception of his beauty and esteem.

Perceiving the wonder of God's glory displayed in the face of Christ gives us the knowledge of who we are in Him— children of glory. We reflect God's image. We are remade in His likeness. When we perceive the face of Jesus shining on us, we cease our search for significance—for we have been found. We are no longer blind.

Take the grace God has given you and give it to yourself. Accept yourself just as you are in your weakness, and you will be lifted up by grace into His peace. If we don't accept ourselves by grace, then that puts us in discord with God. And discord with God is the definition of tension and stress. Give yourself grace through acceptance. We have the ultimate identity in the whole created order.

We also have the ultimate social identity group—the Father, the Son, and the Holy Spirit. We were baptized into His name which symbolizes our acceptance into this fellowship. We have become a part of the Body of Christ and a communion of saints.

We enjoy this in the Father, Son, and Holy Spirit forevermore—heavenly harmony and peace. That identity is bedrock. You are unshakably, unchangeably, and eternally a precious child of God in Christ. You belong to God and His forever family.

The False Self

If we keep striving to reach our own self-generated identity, we will consistently be worried and ever thinking, "Am I enough?" There is no peace in striving to be someone we are not.

A false self is "who we think we are" or would prefer to be. It's an ego. Thomas Merton wrote, "We have the choice of two identities: the external mask which seems to be real...and the hidden, inner person who seems to us to be nothing, but who can give himself eternally to the truth in whom he subsists."[24]

---

[24] Thomas Merton Quotes, Good Reads, www.goodreads.com

That "inner person who seems to be nothing" is who God knows and loves. God does not know the ego because He didn't create it—we did. It's a mental construct. It gets bruised easily. It has no substance.

In response to our nothingness, we strove to make our self to be something. This is smoke. It takes us further away from our true humble self who has been restored by grace.

God created and redeemed the real you, and though you were fallen in sin and failings, He loves you just as you are and gave Himself up for you. To know peace, we must lay aside any vestige of pride and accept this humble, flawed, real self. We can't be lifted without first coming to our senses and realizing we are nothing on our own.

The false, prideful self is easily shaken and knocked off its pedestal. But our new self in Christ cannot be moved. Why? It's grounded in reality. Shed the ego and put on the new self, created in the image and likeness of God.

The Importance of Simply Being

We are first and foremost human beings, not human actors. Working to attain our false identity is inherently stressful. Working from our true identity is inherently holy.

We are God's "holy ones." The Bible never refers to believers as sinners. When sinners are saved by grace, they receive the righteousness of Christ. They are a saint or "holy one" in Him. It's a supreme gift—a pauper becomes a child of the King. This is our true identity.

I've known many Christians who have head knowledge of their new identity but not heart knowledge. Our new identity must be known or experienced in the heart.

Look at yourself just as you are and accept yourself unconditionally in the love of Christ. Accept yourself completely—faults, failures, and all—in the guilt-vanquishing love of Jesus. Accept yourself in your frailty, poverty, and nothingness. And be made rich in Christ.

It's humbling but at the same time uplifting because you come back to your real self. God's grace takes over there. He's got the real you now.

His grace then infuses you with an esteeming love filled with God's strong and shining favor. It's an unmerited favor that lifts the soul to God and anchors you in Christ. He gives you His name and His likeness.

If you are religious, let go of a law-based identity in favor of a grace-based identity. You will have God's righteousness conferred upon you as a gift. True righteousness is sourced in God alone. Then you will shine and beam with your new identity.

That's why Jesus said, "You are the light of the world" (Matthew 5:14). Anyone ever called you by such a lofty title? Me either. But Jesus calls you that. It's who you are in Him, so "let your light shine before others, that they may see your good deeds and glorify your Father in heaven" (Matthew 5:16). We live *from* our new identity, not to *form* one.

My Difficult Journey to Acceptance

When I peeled off all the layers of my pride in prayer and came to my frail and humble self, God hugged me like the prodigal come home. He embraced me. This became ground zero—bedrock identity—for me a sinner, raised to new life, and given His image as a son.

Accepting ourselves in Christ is actually a very difficult transaction to make in our heart even as a Christian. It was difficult for the prodigal too. When he started home, he knew that he didn't belong at the family table anymore. He was unworthy because of what he had done. He had come to his senses—to his real, humble self. He would eat with the servants.

But the prodigal was surprised—probably shocked when he was still a long way off. He looked on the horizon and beheld the father running toward him smiling. His father embraced him completely and kissed him. He called for the ring and the robe. There would be a celebration in the father's house for this one who was dead and now alive again.

Could you allow yourself to be welcomed back home like that by your heavenly Father—with a beaming smile, a welcoming embrace, and a joyful kiss? We are all prodigals.

It seemed wrong to the older brother. He couldn't accept it. Lavish grace just doesn't seem right. It doesn't seem justified. It's so undeserved.

One of the most difficult things I have ever done as a believer was to accept my homecoming to the Father's house. I had been a Christian for years and a pastor for fifteen. I had been a prodigal who came to his senses.

I came back, but mentally I lived in the servant quarters. I felt comfortable there. I loved serving.

But during one season of my life, I, too, was surprised by the Father, who called me up to His house to live as a son—to sit at the table with *my* Father, the Son, and the Holy Spirit. It was an awesome invitation. I knew it, but with every fiber of my being, I also knew I didn't belong there.

I just couldn't do it. It seemed so wrong to have someone like me sit there with them. I knew the terrible things I had done and had failed to do.

But in prayer, I knew God was calling me to come take my seat at His table as a beloved son. I was struggling. I didn't think I could.

Then I saw a bicycle flash into my mind. I thought, "Why am I thinking about this bicycle in this holy moment?" Every time I would dismiss the thought, it would return.

It wasn't just any bicycle; it was the *best* bicycle. I recently had signed up to do an Ironman® Triathlon. I didn't have a bike back then, so I had been searching for a Time-Trial bike to ride the 112-mile bicycle leg of the race.

I was looking to buy a low-priced one to fit my limited budget and ability. But God brought this red and white, best Time Trial bike in the world to my mind while I was struggling with sitting at His table. I tried shaking it off, but the image kept coming back.

Finally, I asked, "God, what are you saying?" He replied, "I want you to buy this bike for your race as My gift to you." I was shocked. I felt like what He was calling me to do was wrong. It was too much money for a mid-life, middle-of-the-pack guy on a very limited budget.

I would never do such a thing. It wasn't prudent. It wasn't appropriate. It went against what I believed to be right.

As I struggled, I started crying as it began to dawn on me. God wanted me to make this transaction in my heart for Him, buy the bike, accept my new identity in Christ, and take my seat at His table.

God wanted me to accept this ring and robe and receive His complete acceptance, not as a servant but as His child. Buying the bike as a gift from Him would be the symbol of this inner spiritual transaction.

I now understood the magnitude of grace. It went against the principle of justice except for one thing—the precious blood of Jesus poured out on Calvary paid the price for a wretched sinner like me to become a son. His love broke my heart. What had seemed a waste of money now seemed like a dignifying grace.

This one transaction would take all our savings. After explaining it to Dana and receiving her support, I did what I would have never otherwise done. I made the transaction and purchased the best bicycle in the world as a gift from God.

As I rode the bike, I thought about what the transaction cost God to have me at His table. It cost God everything. God's house was emptied of His Son to purchase my pardon, restore His image in me, and seat me at His table.

As I write about this, my heart is still affected deeply by it. I wasn't a fast biker. I wasn't a high finisher. I was a struggler. But my Father wanted a lowly sinner to ride the best that day as a word from Him about how He felt about me.

I humbly accepted. Through my tears, I also said to Him, "I'll ride for You wherever You want me to go—even to the ends of the earth."

In my heart, I took His hand and walked up the hill to my Father's house. He opened the door, and I took my seat around His table with the Father, and Son, and the Holy Spirit.

It is the ultimate privilege, the highest honor, the greatest love I have ever known to "be seated with Christ in the heavenly places" (Ephesians 2:6). It's also the most humbling thing I have ever done.

You may be where I was—there on the property serving the Father—but you are not all the way home. Now our Father wants you to accept your place in His house.

It's your turn. You have been living in the servants' quarters too long. It's time to put on the robe, wear the ring, and sit at the Father's table with the Father, His Son Jesus, and the Holy Spirit. It's where you belong.

A Prayer of Acceptance

Maybe the Lord has touched you and wants you to pause and come all the way home right now. His arms are stretched wide, and He invites you to come. If this is you, then this prayer may help you make the transaction in your heart.

"Dear Father, I come back to myself by laying aside my pride and all my failed efforts. I lay them down. It was only a covering, like a fig leaf hiding my shame. I come back to my nothingness.

"Lord Jesus, even now, poor in spirit, I sense Your Presence, holding me close, allowing me to cry out my sin and my shame. You are drawing it out of me, and as it comes out, You are casting it as far as east is from west.

You are my Redeemer. I feel Your grace in my weakness drawing me, lifting me to Yourself. Dear Lord Jesus, I accept myself because You accepted me in all my sin, frailty, and failure.

"Father, I come to you as that prodigal expecting to be treated as a house servant, but I see You running toward me with a smile. I am surprised by Your embrace—how warm and welcoming.

In Your strong hug, I feel that You want me—even me. It feels so good in my soul to be wanted like that. I let Your love and acceptance seep into my being. The ring and the robe, the sandals, and the celebration will mark this new beginning in grace for me. It's all a grace. And I am all Yours."

Just sit for a moment in the presence of God taking in His love for you. Let this be a place you come back to—to remember who you are now and where God brought you from. That will keep you grounded in your new identity.

What About Works?

Works are vitally important but can be a big source of stress if our underlying motive for them is out of harmony with the good news. The following two verses describe the peaceful link between the gospel and works:

"For it is by grace you have been saved, through faith—and this is not from yourselves, it is the gift of God— not by works, so that no one can boast. For we are God's handiwork, created in Christ Jesus to do good works, which God prepared in advance for us to do" (Ephesians 2:8–10).

We do good deeds *because* we are saved, not *to be* saved. We love because God first loved us. We are to be holy because it's who we now are. We serve *from* our new identity, not to *form* an identity. We work because we are His handiwork. We love because we *are* loved, not to get love. We worship not to appease God, but to honor Him. We obey

God not because we "had better or else," but because we want for nothing else.

With grace, Jesus becomes the love of our lives—more precious than life itself. We will do anything for Jesus. He has made His great love for us known to us. He has won us over, and there is none like Him.

Of course we want to please Him with all of our heart, with all of our soul, all of our mind, and all of our strength.

Accepting who we already are by grace is an essential part of being at peace within and ready to love our neighbor as ourselves.

Questions for Reflection and Application

1. "The second is this: 'Love your neighbor as yourself'" (Mark 12:31). Can someone love their neighbor if they reject themselves? Why or why not?

2. Recall the people in your life who gave you unconditional acceptance. Describe how each one affected your life?

3. Who have you loved unconditionally? Write out what that relationship has taught you about love and acceptance.

4. Would you be willing to put aside your pride and honestly look at your true and humble self? If so, what are your failings and weaknesses?

   a. Have you accepted yourself in all your frailties and weaknesses?

   b. Do you feel Jesus accepts you completely just as you are?

   c. Take time in prayer to imagine yourself being hugged by Jesus like the prodigal when he came home. What does that feel like?

   d. Write yourself a letter accepting yourself in God's grace.

Chapter 12

Love Your Neighbor

"So in everything, do to others what you would have them do to you, for this sums up the Law and the Prophets."

MATTHEW 7:12

Isolation from people creates stress and anxiety. Connecting with people fosters peace. We were created for community—with God the Father, the Son, and the Holy Spirit, our neighbors, and our church family. A sense of belonging to God and each other is crucial for a peaceful life.

Believers share a common bond of peace and a dear love for each other—a family love. Our gatherings are to be times of joy and peace together in God's presence.

We are also to be connected with people in the world through the love of Jesus. God loves the world and gives His general grace to everyone—food, water, care, basic needs.

We are not to be unequally yoked together with nonbelievers, but we are to love everyone and contribute to the general welfare of society. We are the salt of the earth. Genuine love connects us with our community.

Love for Our World

It nourishes our soul to help our neighbors, be good citizens, bless our co-workers, greet strangers, volunteer our service...Christians are to be the light of the world. Love connects us to our fellow man.

We also experience God's peace when we live this way. Mother Teresa spoke about this correlation between love and peace when she said, "If we have no peace, it is because we have forgotten that we belong to each other."

Dana and I often eat outside on our front porch in good weather. We see a few neighbors pass by on the sidewalk and wave or chat. We have gotten to know a few of them this way.

It's a throwback to an earlier day in our society—the front porch. We are losing our sense of community in our culture, but some good practices can reconnect us.

Slow Down to Love

We can't be in a hurry and love well. We rush to accomplish tasks when the biggest accomplishments are to be made as we go.

God sets divine appointments that aren't on our list. They don't show up on our calendar. They are not an item on the agenda for our meetings. But God has appointments for us to love our fellow man.

When Jesus taught about the importance of loving our neighbors, someone asked Him, "Who is my neighbor?" Then Jesus told him the parable of the Good Samaritan. That term has come to describe someone in the community who stops to help another person in need regardless of their ethnicity, religion, or political persuasion. The Good Samaritan was traveling, but he stopped, unlike the others, and gave assistance to an unlikely person—a Jew.

John Mark Comer, in his book *The Ruthless Elimination of Hurry,* wrote, "Hurry and love are incompatible. All of my worst moments as a father, a husband, and a pastor, even as a human being, are when I'm in a hurry."[25]

I identify with that quote completely. To live a lifestyle of peace, we have to slow down, practice openness, and take notice of people.

When I visited church members in the hospital or nursing home, there was usually someone else along the way on God's agenda for me to minister to. I often missed those opportunities, but when I did notice and stop, God would move in our lives and bless us. Sometimes, it was the other patient in the room who needed prayer or a healthcare worker who needed encouragement.

---

[25] John Mark Comer, *The Ruthless Elimination of Hurry*, (Colorado Springs: WaterBrook, 2019), 22.

When we slow down and calm ourselves in Christ, we can live by the Spirit and be a blessing as we take care of our responsibilities.

When we scurry and stress, we are living out of our head and in our thoughts. We were made to live from our heart. When we are in a hurry, our mind is frantically thinking about the next task, and our heart isn't engaged. Why? The heart lives in the present. So, we have to slow down to live in love.

Sure, sometimes we have to move quickly but don't let that be your default way of life every day. Build some margin into your day so that you can be present with people.

Collect your thoughts and be at peace as you go. Be interruptible and flexible. Build in some space for divine appointments and walk with God.

What Did Jesus Do?

Jesus "went around doing good" (Acts 10:38). He often stopped as He traveled to a feast or a wedding or some other appointment. He noticed people as He went.

Whether it was a woman at a well who needed some living water, a blind man in need of sight, someone up a sycamore tree who needed to repent, or parents with children who needed a blessing, Jesus stopped to help.

We aren't called to rescue everyone on the street. That's a burden God doesn't place on us. But He will direct our attention and call us to love people as we do life.

In Spirit-led, discerning love, we encourage and help. Love requires the sacrifice of a little time but gives back a whole lot of peace.

My wife attended Western Kentucky University for three consecutive summers to get her master's degree in education. On one such early morning trip on the meandering rural road to school, her car slid into a ditch, and she instantly thought, "Oh, no! What am I going to do? I'm stuck!"

That was before cell phones, but not before Good Samaritans. A repair truck behind her stopped, and two men hopped out and said to Dana, "We will get you out." They hooked her car to a winch, pulled it out of the ditch, and then they were off.

When Dana told me about this later on, I was touched knowing my wife was in distress and two men helped her without hesitation or fanfare. They were on their way to work, and I wanted to let them know how much I appreciated them taking the time to help.

We can't always be there to help our family, but we live in a community where many go about doing good as they do their work. They are called peacemakers.

Let's slow down internally and take a few moments to be there for people along our way.

More Blessed to Give Than Receive

I have seen lives changed from volunteer work done through church to the community and world at large—providing medical care, giving away food, doing disaster relief, providing school supplies, repairing houses…all in Jesus' name with the desire for all to know how much Jesus loves them.

But I think our lives change more than the lives of the people we help. It's the way God works. Peace flows through purpose.

Love gives meaning to life. Love is supreme. Jesus Himself said: "It is more blessed to give than to receive" (Acts 20:35).

The most common Greek word for *blessing* in the New Testament, *makarios*, carries with it the meaning of *reward and happiness*. This is not a worldly, superficial happiness but a deep joy and abiding peace.

Our culture focuses on getting more, but many of us know by experience that it is more blessed to give. Studies show that once people have enough to meet their own basic needs, having more does not result in more happiness.

It's not God's plan for us to focus on our own happiness. A self-centered life isolates us from real community and stifles the flow of God's blessing through us.

Bruce, a friend and father in our church in Roanoke, used to give his kids a hug each day before they departed for work and school. Then he said three things to them, "I love you. You are a blessing, so be a blessing to someone today."

Bruce wanted to imprint these three things in his children. He used an effective practice, a daily habit, to accomplish this goal. He wanted his kids to know they are loved and pass that along to others as they went about their day. They did and still do.

Making a Difference

We are part of the human race, and we have a contribution to make for its general welfare. Through sowing seeds of love, we promote goodwill that ripples through society and affects everyone. Like a pebble tossed into a placid lake, the waves go on forever. Love is eternal. You make a difference through acts of kindness and mercy.

Parents would often ask my coworker Willie to coach their sons' baseball teams. Either as a head coach or an assistant, I watched him shine the light of Jesus and make a big contribution to the development of those boys, including his own.

Willie taught values like how to handle wins and losses, the importance of being a team player, following the rules, shaking off a bad play...This investment of time built character in kids, instilled biblical values, and made family friends for a lifetime.

Many times over the years, I witnessed neighbors taking care of one another during a crisis. One would take out the trash, another mow a lawn, another take kids to school until the crisis was over.

God created us to be interdependent. When neighborhoods are like that, people experience less stress and worry. A peaceful neighborhood sows seeds of trust as they take advantage of times to interact with each other.

When we try to do life on our own, independently in isolation, it backfires. We were made to live in community and serve our neighbors. It wasn't good for man to be alone, and that still holds true today. It gives peace of mind when you are connected to others and have someone you can trust who lives close to you.

Love Begins with Acceptance

God gives us a model for loving the world in the gospel of Christ. Paul wrote: "You see, at just the right time, when we were still powerless, Christ died for the ungodly. Very rarely will anyone die for a righteous person, though for a good person someone might possibly dare to die. But God demonstrates his own love for us in this: While we were still sinners, Christ died for us" (Romans 5:6–8).

While we were unrighteous, Christ showed us His love. He didn't place conditions on it. He didn't require us to reform our ways first. Jesus demonstrated His love for us while we were rebellious and wrong.

This is the basis for demonstrating Christ's love to the world. It starts with accepting people where they are—not requiring them to change or agree with us to be loved by us.

Love begins with acceptance. We are to begin with everyone the same way God began with us—love them where they are without condition. Love starts there.

We are not validating someone's lifestyle by accepting them in love as a fellow human being. Jesus went inside and dined with Matthew's friends who were tax collectors and unrepentant sinners. He didn't judge them, "for God did not send his Son into the world to condemn the world, but to save the world through him" (John 3:17).

The time for judgment will come. But now is not the time, and we are not the judge. We live in the age of grace and are recipients of the unmerited favor of God. We are to give general grace to our fellow man without joining in or condoning their lifestyle. Billy Graham said, "It's the Holy Spirit's job to convict, God's job to judge, and my job to love."

Whiskey Didn't Deter Doug

I drank liquor and got drunk often before coming to Christ. I never thought I would go to church again, but my college roommate compelled me to go one Sunday morning. It went fine. I didn't intend to go back.

But I made a mistake. I filled out a guest card. And someone from church visited me later that week.

When Doug came by, I was surprised. I looked up from my desk and could see him in the doorway. On my desk was a half-empty bottle of whiskey. I looked over the bottle and talked to him. It made me feel uncomfortable.

I watched Doug's eyes and expressions closely as we greeted each other and made small talk. Doug never mentioned the bottle, never even glanced down at it. He did nothing that day but show me acceptance and friendship.

Eventually, that's the very thing that won me over. I could see purity in him and the people from church. They lived the gospel.

I know why Jesus ate with sinners in Matthew's house. It gave them the opportunity to see holiness in the humble heart of Jesus and feel accepted by Him as a person. They hadn't accepted Him yet, but Jesus revealed to them who God was.

The students at church who took me into their fellowship before I was one of them did the same thing for me. They had a nonjudgmental acceptance of me.

They didn't drink with me. They didn't attend my fraternity's parties. But they did share their life with me to the extent they could. They didn't condemn me. That gave me a chance to see Jesus in them.

Their witness validated the gospel for me. If Doug had looked down at that bottle with disdain or made a comment about drinking, I would have closed him down and written him off as one of those hypocrites. But he didn't. He "ate with a sinner," and I've never been the same.

Matthew's friends may never have come into a covenant relationship with Jesus, but they knew they were accepted as a human being and loved. That's where it starts.

Jesus healed everyone brought to Him. He didn't require reformation of character from any of them first. Not everyone became His follower afterwards. But they knew they were loved. This love carries with it the seed of hope and peace.

Mental Walls

Sometimes we build walls in an attempt to keep people we don't like out of our lives, but those walls actually keep those people inside of us. The negative thoughts stay in our heads, and negative emotions seep into our hearts.

When we let down the walls and love those people, these thoughts and emotions leave us. Their power over us is released. Love needs no protection but God. He goes before us and has our back. That's why we can love freely and not require anything in return.

Mental and emotional walls are anxiety-producing factories because fear is the fuel that sustains them. Anxious thoughts are employed as their security guards. They are used for protection in this mindset. It takes energy to keep a mental construct up and working. It's exhausting and wearisome over time.

That is too steep a price for protection—especially when God will protect you and keep you. He is your fortress. Jesus is your sanctuary. His power secures you safe "under the shadow of His wings."

We can have either mental walls or a mighty fortress protecting us, but we can't have both at the same time. A choice for love is a choice for peace.

Hell is where all men are isolated from God and each other. There is no love in hell, therefore there is no connection—only absolute, eternal, walled-off isolation from God and people.

On the cross when Jesus took our place, He felt that separation and estrangement from God that we deserved and cried out, "My God, my God, why have you forsaken me?" (Matthew 27:46).

Heaven is the opposite—God's love bonds us all together in love for Jesus and each other. To choose to love is a choice to advance the Kingdom of heaven.

Walling people out divides our soul and fractures our self into pieces. A little piece of us goes behind every barrier. Isolating our enemy also isolates a part of us. We can't be whole again until our heart opens up to everyone in gospel love. Through Jesus, we can be free to love again.

Wise Boundaries

We need to have wise boundaries in relationships—not mental and emotional walls. Relational boundaries are set with wisdom while walls are erected with fear.

Boundaries in relationships are necessary if we are to accomplish God's purpose for our lives. We cannot say yes to every person or opportunity. We cannot allow other people's agenda to override God's agenda for our life, our family, or ministry.

We will stress out if boundaries are not set. Having a wise boundary with some people doesn't require an emotional barrier. It requires discernment and action.

The criterion we are to use for setting boundaries is God's will. We can find general boundaries for all of God's people in His Word.

For example: "Do not make friends with a hot-tempered person, do not associate with one easily angered, or you may learn their ways and get yourself ensnared" (Proverbs 22:24–25). We are to love "hot-tempered" people but not make friends with them lest we learn their ways.

Hanging out with chronic complainers or drama-making gossips can ensnare us in a web of stress. The Bible clearly calls us to a different conversation infused with faith, hope, and love.

If you can't guide the conversation in that direction, then guide yourself away from close friendship with that person.

Jesus made no time for idle talk with the Pharisees. He loved them but left them to their hypocrisy.

God will make known to you His will in particular situations—who to invest your time in, who to connect with for your own spiritual health, where to serve, who to date, when to leave....

Thomas Aquinas wrote, "To love is to will the good of another." It starts in the heart. We can set boundaries and continue to "will the good" of that person. We can have an open heart of love and a wise walk among men.

Jesus taught, "I am sending you out like sheep among wolves. Therefore be as shrewd as snakes and as innocent as doves" (Matthew 10:16). Boundaries require knowing God's moral wisdom and living from it to fulfill His purpose and plan.

Live with insight on this from His Word. God's peace reigns within the boundaries of this land.

God and Us, Not God and Me

I am continuously transformed by the use of plural pronouns in The Lord's Prayer—*our, us,* and *we* instead of *me* and *my.* This prayer connects me through love with everyone, our world, our family, and our church. Notice these pronouns as Jesus teaches the prayer.

"This, then, is how you should pray: 'Our Father in heaven, hallowed be your name, your kingdom come, your will be done, on earth as it is in heaven. Give us today our daily bread. And forgive us our debts, as we also have forgiven our debtors. And lead us not into temptation, but deliver us from the evil one'" (Matthew 6:9–13).

Praying like this unites us in love for each other. We are in God's kingdom together with our brothers and sisters in Christ. We are also in this world together with everyone.

It's reminiscent of how Paul instructed us to pray: "I urge, then, first of all, that petitions, prayers, intercession and thanksgiving be made for all people—for kings and all those in authority, that we may live peaceful and quiet lives in all godliness and holiness. This is good, and pleases God our Savior, who wants all people to be saved and to come to a knowledge of the truth" (I Timothy 2:1–4).

This is a prayer of love and peace, salvation and truth. Giving thanks for all people helps us realize God's love in our heart for all people. This love is strong—pure and without prejudice. He loves the saved and unsaved.

God is love, and He offers His love to all. He does not delight in the death of the wicked. Ultimately, He "wants all people to be saved and come to a knowledge of the truth."

Love Your Enemies

There are to be no exceptions to love, no passes given for an enemy, no special cases, no one excluded. Love is the gospel. Love is not a secondary issue but an all-encompassing command. To be in harmony with God, we must love everyone, and we can through Jesus.

Jesus taught, "But love your enemies, do good to them, and lend to them without expecting to get anything back. Then your reward will be great, and you will be children of the Most High, because he is kind to the ungrateful and wicked. Be merciful, just as your Father is merciful" (Luke 6:35-36).

We become like God when we are good to our enemies. They will come to know who Jesus is when we love them like He does. The world should identify Christians with love, not a political movement. That will happen when we "are kind to the ungrateful and wicked" and "do good to them" like our heavenly Father.

The people of the world are not our enemies, even though some of them may consider Christians their enemies. We have no enemy but Satan. Our "battle is not against flesh and blood" (Ephesians 6:12).

Good works done in Jesus' name show our enemies that we really do love them, and more importantly, that God loves them. Some of our enemies will even become our friends through this gospel way of living. It's a powerful witness.

Loving our enemies requires prayer. We don't have this capacity in ourselves. We need the Holy Spirit to impart His heroic virtue into our hearts. That starts with prayer. It's the first step of faith. Bring that person to God's throne of grace and pray for them.

Billy Graham said, "You cannot pray for someone and hate them at the same time." The last thing our selfish nature wants to do is pray for our enemy. Our flesh wants to defend ourselves and demand our way.

Personally, if someone upsets me, I have to *make* myself get on my knees and pray for them. I do this against my feelings. I *will myself* to pray for them out of the fear of God. This prayer takes humility but eventually gives peace in return.

So, I get on my knees and pray and keep praying for my enemy until God's love comes to my heart. It works. With a step of faith in obedience to the gospel, the Holy Spirit begins to move. Love and peace will form in us every time we step out in faith to do God's will.

Christ-like love contains no upset, fear, stress, or anxiety. His love, when formed in us, will never fail to bring us peace. If anger for someone returns to my heart, I return to prayer and keep praying until God's love and peace form in me.

How do you pray for enemies? Back when I first started practicing this prayer, I prayed for God to change the person—their misguided, offensive, and hard-hearted ways. But the Holy Spirit wasn't guiding that prayer, and fruit didn't come. It was a Pharisee's prayer.

I sought the Lord, thought about the gospel, and the Word of God came to me about how to pray. In Luke 6:28, Jesus said, "Bless those who curse you, pray for those who mistreat you."

I didn't feel like doing it, but I began to ask God to bless my enemy and their loved ones. To bless means to give favor. I couldn't believe I was asking God to give my enemy His favor. But I kept it up, and the Holy Spirit began to work within me, and I continued to ask God to bless them.

I started experiencing the goodwill of grace that God had for my enemy. Then something surprising happened. They were no longer my enemy. God's love for them had been formed in my heart.

Love overcomes evil. God's love for this world is stronger than any hate could ever be. Pray and bless until love is formed.

Then, when an opportunity to do some little good for our enemy comes up, we will be ready to respond because we have been prepared through prayer. Often, but not always, this act of goodwill can be the beginning of a friendship or a restored friendship.

"There is no fear in love. But perfect love drives out fear..." (I John 4:18). We think that the commands of God are restrictive, but they are freeing. God's commands don't hem us in; they break us free by the working of the Spirit.

God's love is the ultimate spiritual treasure—more precious than any gold or silver.

Love people like Jesus and our fear will be gone. It's supernatural. Pray through what's hard until God's love is formed in your heart. The peace of Jesus is bonded to His love

Loving everyone is a challenge but not an option. If we ignore it, we will be in tension with God and people. Doing good to all sows peace in this world. And our world needs peace.

Peace rides on the coattails of God's *agape* love. When we align our heart with Jesus in His Passion, He lines our heart with peace in our relationships.

Forgive Freely from the Heart

When offended, forgive as God in Christ has forgiven you. Stress will be released, anxiety over the person's actions will vanish, and your body will relax through forgiveness. Nothing you could ever do is more gracious, generous, or central to living out the gospel of Jesus than forgiving someone for their trespasses.

Forgive and be at peace with God, yourself, and your neighbor. Jesus said, "Do not judge, and you will not be judged. Do not condemn, and you will not be condemned. Forgive, and you will be forgiven. Give, and it will be given to you. A good measure, pressed down, shaken together and running over, will be poured into your lap. For with the measure you use, it will be measured to you" (Luke 6:37–38).

Giving mercy to people who have offended you will release a cascade of blessings from heaven and fill your life. God is honored when we forgive because we are choosing to be like Jesus.

We are giving like God gives when we forgive. We will receive back from God much more than we give. Peace of mind will be one of the most precious blessings of giving mercy.

How do we know when we have completely forgiven our offender? Forgive until there is goodwill in your heart toward the one who offended you. Forgive until you can genuinely bless those who persecuted you.

Inner tension releases and anxiety over the offense disappears when we forgive. It takes Christ-like humility, but it reestablishes harmony with God and inner peace with our neighbor. Paul wrote, "If it is possible, as far as it depends on you, live at peace with everyone" (Romans 12:18).

It also is the first step, and sometimes the only step necessary, to reconcile with someone. Reconciliation is a process where trust must be restored between two parties. Sometimes trust needs to be rebuilt over time with deeds that reflect a change in the offending person. In any event, forgiveness is always the first step.

Give the gift of forgiveness unilaterally, regardless of the condition of the offender—repentant or unrepentant, dead or alive. Make the transaction through prayer.

1. Be angry because of their sin against you. (Ephesians 4:26, ESV)
2. Let the anger go to Jesus.
3. Cancel their debt.
4. Release them to God.

Through forgiveness, people will be disempowered from holding emotional sway over you. The devil will shrink back. Stress will be relieved. Your mind will become tranquil. It will humble you and bring you near to God.

Forgiveness by grace is the central tenet of our faith. We will need to practice forgiveness many times throughout life. God commands it. We cannot move forward without it.

Forgiveness is more powerful than holding on to the offense. Love "keeps no record of wrongs...Love never fails" (I Corinthians 13:5–8). You can trust this act of obedience to lead you in the way of Jesus, the way everlasting and the way of peace.

The Way of Peace

"Blessed are the peacemakers, for they will be called children of God" (Matthew 5:9). We have been given the ministry of reconciliation and peace for the world. The world responded to Jesus in various ways. We can expect similar responses.

We can plant seeds for reconciliation only through living out the gospel. The following Christian "Prayer of Peace" highlights the lifestyle of a peacemaker:

Lord, make me an instrument of your peace:
where there is hatred, let me sow love;
where there is injury, pardon;
where there is doubt, faith;
where there is despair, hope;
where there is darkness, light;
where there is sadness, joy.
O divine Master, grant that I may not so much seek
to be consoled as to console,
to be understood as to understand,
to be loved as to love.
For it is in giving that we receive,
it is in pardoning that we are pardoned,
and it is in dying that we are born to eternal life.
Amen.

Love Your Spiritual Family

You belong to God and His forever family. You are a child of the Father and a brother or sister to many. The church is not a building but a fellowship of people redeemed by the blood of Jesus. We belong to each other. Everyone is important.

When we commit ourselves to God's family, we get connected to a vital source of spiritual power. God works through His church to build us up in Christ. John Donne wrote, "No man is an island."

When we try to live out our walk with God without being connected to His Body, we will soon become weak. Stress and worry will become more prevalent because we have isolated ourselves from a vital source of spiritual renewal.

We need our spiritual family. Without them, we are like a sailboat without the wind. We need each other to make headway on our journey with God.

Paul wrote, "The eye cannot say to the hand, 'I don't need you!' And the head cannot say to the feet, 'I don't need you!' On the contrary, those parts of the body that seem to be weaker are indispensable" (I Corinthians 12:21–22).

God uses "what *seems* to be weaker" as indispensable is His plan. It's His way. I have witnessed this many, many times. Children, the physically or mentally challenged, prodigals, people with checkered pasts…. I could go on and on as I think about the tremendous spiritual impact some people who are deemed by the world as "weaker" have had in the Body of Christ.

One of those is twelve-year-old Abbey. She is a special girl in our church fellowship in Roanoke. Every time she sees one of her friends, she lights up like a Christmas tree and greets them with a hug.

When she saw me, she would start walking quickly toward me, saying, "Pastor Jake, Pastor Jake!" She would give me a big hug, take me by the arm, and say, "Come sit with us. Sing with us. Where is Dana?" I knew that Jesus was using Abbey to make us all feel dearly loved.

Use your gifts to serve in the Body of Christ. God has given us His Holy Spirit and has endowed us with gifts to use to build up others and His family, the church.

People thrive when they find their God-given place of service. They come alive and desire to do this work because the Holy Spirit works through them to make an eternal difference. We experience the peace of God when we are doing what God redeemed us to do.

Paul and the believers he served had a strong bond and affection for each other. They shared in God's grace and peace. Paul wrote, "I have you in my heart." If we bond to God's people, we will find a source of strength and courage that comes from God.

Our unity is in the bond of peace. We must be eager to promote peace and careful to protect it. Love knits our hearts together in God's family. The following verse tells us what aspects of love are essential to deepen and protect this pleasant peace and joy of the saints.

Paul wrote: "Be completely humble and gentle; be patient, bearing with one another in love. Make every effort to keep the unity of the Spirit through the bond of peace" (Ephesians 4:2–3).

Patience in a family is important for lasting peace. Everyone has their ways, opinions, and eccentricities. We have to bear with each other.

If we lose patience with each other, our unity will be fragile. The first word Paul uses to describe godly love is "Love is patient…" (I Corinthians 13:4).

Suffering long with someone is part of a godly and peaceful nature. God suffered long for us. His patience and kindness led us to repentance. God is patient, so He expects His children to be. When people get out of sorts, say the wrong thing, or get upset, be patient.

"If it weren't for people, my job would be great." I've heard that phrase more than a few times over the years, but never really believed it. I realized in my own journey that people aren't usually the problem.

We must reframe our view of some "difficult people" to see the problem a little differently. Love is patient. So, is a difficult person causing my stress or is my lack of patience stressing me out?

People are going to be people. We are not perfect. With patience we can learn how to love each other. And real patience is really peaceful. Patience is a core characteristic of peace-makers. A sense of inner calm is present when handling issues.

Let's practice being patient by inwardly letting go of our willful desires in order to give people and God time to work it out. This self-denial will dignify the person and honor God.

Accept Your Brother in Christ

Even Christians disagree. We can't back away from a relationship every time someone posts something we don't like on social media. We must accept the brother or sister who doesn't see a matter like we do if it is not essential to salvation or basic morality. Just let it go and love them.

Paul addressed drinking wine, special holy days, and eating meat in a fellowship of people with Jewish and pagan backgrounds. That social mix was a recipe for disunity.

But Paul gave them gospel commands on how to treat each other. He didn't tell them how to believe on each matter. He wrote how to practice peace when disputable matters or opinions are being addressed.

He taught us to, "Accept the one whose faith is weak, without quarreling over disputable matters. One person's faith allows them to eat anything, but another, whose faith is weak, eats only vegetables. The one who eats everything must not treat with contempt the one who does not, and the one who does not eat everything must not judge the one who does, for God has accepted them. Who are you to judge someone else's servant? To their own master, servants stand or fall. And they will stand, for the Lord is able to make them stand" (Romans 14:1–4).

There are matters of conscience that each person must address for themselves after a careful study of the Scripture. They are not essential to our salvation, but they are important. We have to decide about them as we follow Christ.

Settle those issues between you and the Lord using the Bible as your guide. Then follow your conscience. Be discerning about such matters, but let others have their freedom. Don't cause your brother to stumble.

If the potential for discord exists, then keep what you believe about such matters between you and God. That is a wise and peaceful response.

Therefore, Paul writes in this context: "So whatever you believe about these things keep between yourself and God. Blessed is the one who does not condemn himself by what he approves" (Romans 14:22).

We need to make every effort to do what leads to peace and mutual edification. We can be in one accord with God and at peace with our brother when we keep some things to ourselves. The closeness and sweetness of fellowship in the unity of the Spirit is to be safeguarded.

True Wisdom Has a Peace-loving Nature

James writes, "But the wisdom that comes from heaven is first of all pure; then peace-loving, considerate, submissive, full of mercy and good fruit, impartial and sincere. Peace-

makers who sow in peace reap a harvest of righteousness"
(James 3:17–18).

Wisdom from heaven is not forceful. It is submissive. It
is not demanding but considerate. It's not corrupted but
pure, not judgmental but full of mercy. This unifies families
and churches.

People of godly character can influence others to godliness by modeling this wisdom. When we act with this nature,
God's will is discerned and a harvest of righteousness is
reaped in due season. Blessed are the peacemakers.

In essential matters, let there be unity. In everything else,
let there be freedom of conscience and respect for our brothers for whom Christ gave His life. Let the small stuff go and
be at peace.

Encouragement

Encouragement is a great stress relief. Sometimes I arrived to
church on Sunday morning feeling stressed. It started on
Saturday night thinking my sermon was not good enough,
not brief enough, not powerful…and those negative thoughts
would often still be with me after my morning prayer. By the
time I got to church, I felt a real battle.

But as I headed for the pulpit at the 8:00 a.m. service,
almost without fail, a brother or sister in Christ would greet
me with a smile or give me a hug. When that happened, the
battle was over, the devil was defeated, and a right spirit was

set in me. I regularly experienced the power of a Spirit-filled, loving fellowship that passed the peace.

I began to reflect on this dynamic. What was happening as I walked to the pulpit? God's love was being reflected to me by His children. Their smiles and greetings, their embraces, and their words were all reflections of God's affection and support of me.

Everyone needs the Body of Christ. We all benefit as we liberally give God's love and encouragement to each other.

Our Fellowship

We are on a Pilgrim journey together through a desert to get to the Promised Land of heaven. God, our Good Shepherd, is with us.

Gather with God's people. Commit and get connected. Stay flocked up in meaningful relationships and service. Don't regularly miss the blessed gatherings of God's family for worship.

Fellowship in small group Bible studies is essential to forming this bond of peace. The gates of hell will not prevail against God's church. Even if one sheep does go astray, the Good Shepherd will go and work to bring them back into the fold.

On our own, we fall prey to the wolves. Together in Christ, we are spiritually secure. We were made for this special fellowship.

Everywhere I have lived, I have found Bible-based fellowships of true believers who helped me stay anchored in Jesus and experience the love and peace He gives.

Seek God First

"It had been five years since I had asked someone for a date, but at age twenty-five, I tried again. I was so nervous. Finally, I got up the nerve to dial Dana's number and ask if she wanted to go out for dinner. To my relief, she said yes.

We went to a Greek restaurant in Lusaka, Africa, and enjoyed our evening. I'll never forget it. She ordered fish that, when it came, still had the head on it.

We dated, but she thought it was just for friendship because I never even held her hand. She had no idea I was serious about her until we went on an outing with a group of missionaries to see Victoria Falls and do some whitewater rafting down the Zambezi River below.

The rafting was going great until our raft capsized, and we were all dumped into the class IV rapids of the mighty Zambezi. I tried in vain to swim to the surface, thinking to myself all the while, "I'm going to drown, and she will never know I love her."

Thankfully, I finally surfaced and instantly looked around to see if Dana was safe. To my relief, I spotted her sitting on top of the overturned raft and decided at that moment, "Tonight's the night."

Our entire missionary group went out that night and sat around a large round table eating and reminiscing about our eventful day. As the evening wound down, I looked across the table and said, "Dana, bwerani kuno?" I smiled at her as I rose and began walking away and glancing back as I did.

The missionaries, who knew the language, told Dana, "He wants you to walk with him." They were laughing, thinking it quite humorous, which I intended it to be.

Dana rose and joined me on the road by the Falls. As we walked, I knew the moment had come, so I looked at her and said, "Dana, I need to let you know something." I paused, then said, "I love you."

I said it, and it felt great! I waited anxiously for her response, but I could tell she was shocked. I was shocked that she was shocked. Then, she looked up at me and very sincerely said, "Thank you." I thought, *Thank you?*

I didn't see Dana over the next two or three weeks. There was nothing more I could say. I was preparing to leave with my friend, Marlin, to do some sightseeing in Asia and Australia on our way back to the States. However, Dana was constantly on my mind.

One Friday after work, I returned to the Baptist Student Center, where I lived in a room in the back of the building. My friend Phiri greeted me and told me that Miss Dana had come by earlier and dropped off a letter.

He handed it to me, and my heart immediately jumped into my throat. I returned to my room and opened it, finding a typed missive about seven pages long. *Not good,* I thought. I read through it as fast as I could and, reaching the very end, I read, "…and I love you, too."

Hallelujah! She loves me too!

My future wife from Minnesota was found by a native Virginian in Africa as we both were seeking first "God's kingdom and his righteousness" (Matthew 6:33), not the next person to date." [26]

This holds true for having the peace of Christ. If we seek peace for its own sake, it will elude us. When we seek first the kingdom of God and His righteousness, God's peace will be given to us (Matthew 6:33). This principle was taught by Jesus in the context of His command for us to not worry about our life. God is faithful. He will provide.

Dana has come full circle now. She's back in Minnesota. We feel blessed to be here sharing life with her parents.

A Prayer for You

When our church didn't gather for a few weeks in the early days of the pandemic, I wanted to stay close to the people in my church family the way Paul did while he was away or in prison.

He had them in his heart and gave thanks to God for them as he remembered them with joy in prayer before the Lord. I did that and was able to be with my brothers and sis-

---

[26] Excerpted from my book, *Transformed Through Trials,* 18–19.

ters in spirit through prayer. I felt the endearing spiritual connection even though we were not physically with each other.

In a similar way, I feel that fellowship with you. We have journeyed together through the pages of this book.

It's been a heart-felt privilege for me to have had this seat at your table. As we close, this is my prayer for you: "The LORD bless you and keep you; the LORD make his face shine on you and be gracious to you; the LORD turn his face toward you and give you peace" (Numbers 6:24-26). God bless you dear friend.

Thank you for reading my book. I hope something in it has blessed you. If you feel comfortable, please consider leaving a review on Amazon. A sentence or two from you might point someone else in the right direction.

Questions for Reflection and Application

1. "But God demonstrates his own love for us in this: While we were still sinners, Christ died for us" (Romans 5:8).

   a. Since Christ died for us while we were still sinners, how should we show Christ's love to the world?

   b. Who showed you acceptance when you needed it the most? What did they do to make you feel accepted and loved?

   c. Why was that so important to you at that time in your life?

2. Do you feel connected to the people in your neighborhood? List three things you could do to form better relationships with your neighbors.

3. What talents do you have that you could use to be a Good Samaritan and help someone in distress?

   a. When has a Good Samaritan helped you or a family member?

   b. Describe what that was like.

4. Do you have someone you would call an enemy? Someone you harbor ill will toward? Write their name(s).

   a. Are you ready to forgive them? If so, use the following steps to form your thoughts into a prayer of forgiveness.

- Be angry because of their sin against you. (Ephesians 4:26, ESV)
- Let the anger go to Jesus.
- Cancel their debt.
- Release them to God.

b. Write a prayer of forgiveness. Express the wrong done. Describe it and how it made you feel. Cancel the debt and release the wrongdoer to Jesus who paid that debt. Put the person in God's hands.

5. What attributes are needed to be patient with our brothers and sisters in Christ?

a. What divisive topics sometimes come up in Christian conversations?

b. What topics of Christian conversation would this verse apply to? "So whatever you believe about these things keep between yourself and God. Blessed is the one who does not condemn himself by what he approves" (Romans 14:22).

6. "There is no fear in love" (I John 4:18). What does this verse mean to you?

a. How have you experienced it as true?

b. Who are you having trouble loving?

c. Write out a prayer of blessing for them.

7. What practices from this book do you feel motivated to apply to your life?

   a. Write out a plan to help you develop these practices into life-changing habits.

   b. Who could you ask to encourage you or join you in following these practices?

Acknowledgments

I couldn't have made it for thirty years as the lead pastor of two churches without a lot of grace and patience from the wonderful people I served. Thank you, Corinth Baptist and Villa Heights Baptist, our church family for over thirty years! You encouraged us and supported us through the calm and through the storm. I am so grateful for each person. We grew very close as we shared life together in Christ. I look forward to God's big family reunion when we can recount the many awesome works God did in our midst. We miss you terribly and love you dearly.

Thank you to our incredible family for all of your love, support, and prayers. We love our vacations together, video calls, and staying in touch with all that's going on in your lives. You bless us so much!

Over the last year, Dana and I have been enriched by Berean Baptist Church in Burnsville, Minnesota. They have welcomed us as one of their own. The Discovery Class has become like family to us. We love serving Jesus with a church so alive in Christ!

Thank you, Art and Connie, for the feedback you provided on this book. I appreciate your wisdom.

Thank you Peter and Carol for the final edits!

Thank you to all my prayer partners and pre-readers!

Also Available

by Jake Huffman

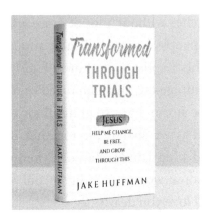

Learn how to grow when life gets hard. Pastor Jake's transparency and real-life applications of the Word will help you experience goodness of God in any trial.

About the Author

Pastor Jake Huffman and his wife Dana served two thriving churches for thirty years, at Villa Heights Baptist in Roanoke, Virginia, and Corinth Baptist in McQuady, Kentucky. He and the people he served grew together as they applied biblical principles to life's everyday challenges.

Jake was raised in Richlands, Virginia, and received a BS in Commerce from the University of Virginia and a Master of Divinity from the Southern Baptist Theological Seminary.

In addition to writing and speaking, Jake enjoys hiking and biking with Dana and vacations with his family. They now reside near Dana's parents in Apple Valley, Minnesota.

Printed in Great Britain
by Amazon

26766258R00162